INVESTMENT COMMITTEE GUIDE TO PRUDENCE

Increasing the Odds of Success When Fulfilling Your Fiduciary Responsibilities in the Administration of Pension/Investment Assets

JONATHAN J. WOOLVERTON, CFA

The Investment Committee Guide to Prudence

Tellwell Talent
www.tellwell.ca

ISBN
978-0-2288-6160-7 (Hardcover)
978-0-2288-6159-1 (Paperback)
978-0-2288-6161-4 (eBook)

A comprehensive review of the duties, responsibilities, and roles of investment committees, including plan sponsors and investors, that are responsible for the safe-keeping, administration, and management of the plan's investable assets. The primary focus is on prudence and best practices when acting as a fiduciary responsible to plan beneficiaries.

To Family

ACKNOWLEDGMENTS

I developed an interest in the investment field by chance. I was entering my fourth year of university seeking a major in economics and accounting, with a minor in psychology, with virtually no idea what career path to take. My business courses did not inspire me, and I wondered if I was wasting money on further education. At the start of my senior year, when my school was unable to offer its regular course in economics, my guidance counselor substituted a course on investing instead. For the university, this was a new, relatively uncharted field, and, therefore, the course was not well attended—providing me with a lot of quality professor time. Three weeks into this course, I had finished reading all the course material and began seeking out more information. I was hooked. I went to my professor and asked for further reading material. At that time, very little had been written on investing or about the investment industry in general (it was the mid-1960s). I gathered what I could find—including the seminal 1947 text, *The Intelligent Investor* by Benjamin Graham. Looking back, this course was life-changing. From that moment on, I could not get enough information about this new field. I tell my kids and grandkids that I have put in 50- to 60-hour weeks for the past 50 years yet have not had to work a day in my life. My entry into the investment field quickly became a career.

One of the greatest privileges I have had within the investment community is the number of highly intelligent, highly motivated, thought-provoking professionals that I have come across from within plan sponsor organizations, the investment management community, and investment planning consulting firms. Many have shaped who I am today and made me a better money manager and investment planning consultant along the way.

Two investment planning professionals (both with actuarial backgrounds—which I do not hold against them) have had a significant impact on my investment consulting career and on the creation of this book. The first is

Don Ezra, without whose urging, encouragement, and, basically, nagging, this book would not have been written. Don is a former co-chairperson of a large global investment planning consulting firm. Just over a year ago, I was writing an article for an investment magazine and asked him to review it before publication. I had been asked to write a 12- to 15-page article on investment manager selection for this magazine and got a little carried away—to the extent of an additional 30 pages. This was far too lengthy for the publication. I then asked Don if he would be willing to condense the article to fit the magazine's requirements. Don said that I was well on my way to writing a book—and that I should continue. It took me about a year to write, and my family is still not talking to Don. Over his career, Don has had a major influence on the global pension and investment communities. His insights into this book have been invaluable.

The second person who assisted me significantly with this book is Colin Carlton. Colin provided additional wisdom to refine the concepts and ideas outlined in many chapters and challenged my assumptions every step of the way. He has been a major contributor to both the pension and investment fields and is a highly respected investment planning specialist. Colin is an internal consultant to one of the largest investment funds in North America, providing strategic inputs into the fund's decision-making process.

I have known Don and Colin for most of my working career. Every time I sat down with either of them, I learned something new, or my knowledge was expanded to grasp an emerging concept or idea. Don and Colin would anticipate trends in the fields of investing and consulting long before they occurred. Both are at the top of my list of the most intelligent professionals I have come across within the pension and investment fields. I cannot thank them enough for their assistance with this book. Both have written articles and spoken at many conferences, and Don has written a number of books on the pension industry (I have lost count of how many). My life has been enriched by their friendship. Thank you.

Other professionals who have had a major impact on my career include Michael Barkley (who continues to lead the way in providing high-quality servicing to private wealth clients), Tom Bradley (who embodies the definition of integrity), and George Mavroudis (a continuing example of principled-centered leadership).

I have been a member of CFA Institute for well over four decades. This organization has had a major influence on both the pension and investment communities. CFA Institute plays a major role in setting a high standard of ethical conduct and behavior for investment professionals, and provides ongoing education to its members on the industry's current topics and trends. The organization is invaluable to the investment community. I thank CFA Institute for consistently challenging investment professionals to always operate in the best interests of their clients.

TABLE OF CONTENTS

APPENDICES

1. Code of Conduct, Ethics, and Confidentiality Policy
2. Investment Policy & Procedures Statement: Outline
3. U.S.: Yearly Rates of Change
4. Canada: Yearly Rates of Change
5. Investment Management Agreement: Outline
6. Trade and Brokerage Allocation Policy: Sample
7. Proxy Voting Policy: Sample
8. Investment Committee Mandate Statement: Outline
9. Investment Management Evolution

INTRODUCTION

The investment committee may be the most important committee within any plan sponsor or other investment-type organization.

In their role as trustees, fiduciaries, and administrators, the members of investment committees *must* operate in the best interest of all plan beneficiaries. The *plan sponsor and investor*, typically, has the administrative role of outlining the types of authorities, responsibilities, and accountabilities of the various service providers (e.g., actuarial and consulting firms, investment management organizations, custodians, and performance measurement firms) that interact with pension or investment funds. The *investment committee* is charged with the responsibility for creating and implementing the investment program and seeking out the service providers required to administer and manage the various investment funds. The committee is typically supported by internal investment staff members who are responsible for overseeing, monitoring, and evaluating all fund activities.

Throughout this book I will use the term *plan sponsor* to represent the collective of the various entities (i.e., corporations, government bodies, institutions, foundations, charitable organizations, and mutual funds) that have the fiduciary responsibility to oversee, administer, manage, and monitor investment funds on behalf of fund beneficiaries and other end users.

The investment committee has three main functions:

1. *return*: to create an investment program to achieve the goals and objectives of the fund as a whole;

2. *risk*: to determine the risk parameters (i.e., the ability and willingness to tolerate the risks involved in achieving the desired return objectives); and,

3. *cost*: to ensure that the overall costs of implementing the investment program are reasonable, given the expected outcome.

The investment committee's fiduciary responsibility presents challenges for committee members. Because money management may be the most uncertain business in the world, the most important decisions that investment committee members make are in selecting and weighting various asset classes (known as the *asset mix policy*). The asset mix policy is based on forecasts of the longer-term rates of return for the various components of the capital market, the volatility of the returns of each asset class, and the correlations of one asset class to another.

For investment committee members, the investment business hinges on beliefs about the following questions:

- Will the components of the capital market behave as they have in the past, given the historical relationships between return, volatility, and correlations?

- What is the expected inflation rate for the next 20 or so years, and how will this forecast affect the anticipated fund results?

- If choosing active management and investment strategies, can investment managers deliver cost-effective, above-benchmark returns as in the past or as promised, and do committee members have the experience and skill to select these managers?

From the investment side, money management firms operate in an environment of incomplete information. The markets are driven by events that are somewhat random and, as a result, unpredictable.

In summary, all major decisions that the investment committee members are going to make are based, mainly, on uncertainty.

Pensions and other types of investment funds are now big business. They have all the necessary features of any other division of a corporate or governing body. As a result, plan sponsors must gather the professional resources needed to ensure that the overall goals and objectives are met. A fund can no longer be administered and managed on a part-time basis. Most defined-benefit pension plans possess unique features of being long-term and having positive (and relatively consistent, stable, and predictable) cash flows. In the vast majority of cases, the investment committee members have the luxury of investing for the long run.

This book is not intended to provide all (or even any) of the answers to investing in the capital market, as each plan sponsor (whether a pension fund, an operating or endowment fund, a charitable organization, a foundation, or a financial institution) has different beliefs, risk tolerances and appetites, and investment goals and objectives. However, hopefully, readers will get a deeper understanding of how the investment community works and the incentives inherent within the various service providers that may create unacceptable biases and conflicts. One of the goals of this book is to provide questions that investment committee members should ask of their service providers to increase the odds of success. Above all else, members should remember the power of compound interest that we all learned in school—and, thus, focus less on short-term thinking and more on delivering longer-term results. The entire focus of the investment committee members should be on making informed judgments.

The investment fund sponsor, the investment planning consultant and actuary, and investment management professionals all begin their processes with a set of "beliefs." The main belief of plan sponsors is that they can formulate the optimal risk/reward balance (although there really is no such thing, only the illusion of optimality) to deliver promises made to the plan beneficiaries of their investment funds. Plan sponsors must also believe that they have the skills needed to hire the required internal resources and engage external service providers to achieve these goals and objectives. Without an efficient and effective process, there is a risk that plan contributions would have to be increased significantly for the plan sponsor or current plan participants, or that benefits would have to be reduced significantly. The primary focus is to ensure that the *promises* made to the beneficiaries are achieved.

The belief of the actuary and investment planning consultant is that they can provide a service to enhance the fund return as a whole and/or reduce the overall level of risk to the fund of the plan sponsor. In addition, investment planning consultants believe that they possess sufficiently in-depth knowledge of the pension and investment fields to provide their clients with the necessary education to be "best-in-class" fiduciaries.

Active investment managers believe they can add value through a disciplined decision-making process that gives them an edge over other money managers operating within the same space. Given this advantage, they believe that they can outperform the specific benchmarks used to measure their success.

The size of the investment fund will also dictate, to some extent, the investment options available to investment committees. Mega pension and investment funds may believe that building an investment team internally is the most effective way to achieve their own goals and objectives. Mid-size funds may prefer a more hybrid structure in which some monies are managed internally, with, maybe, non-traditional asset classes managed by external money managers. Smaller investment funds, typically, have external investment managers to manage all their assets and internal investment staff to oversee and monitor ongoing investment fund activities. Plan sponsors of smaller funds may also outsource the entire money management function to an investment management platform. These platforms are usually designed to provide for appropriate diversification through investment managers within selected asset classes with complementary investment styles. The good news is that, with all the investment products and vehicles available to plan sponsors in today's environment, the larger funds no longer have the size advantage that they once had.

Broadly, there are four types of stakeholders with an interest in the various pension and investment funds:

1. *current plan participants* (who expect promises to be kept);

2. *retirees* (who hope that inflation will not erode their income stream);

3. the *plan sponsor* (which attempts to keep contributions as low as possible); and,

4. if the fund is sponsored by a public corporation, the *shareholder* (which expects company management to focus on enhancing share value).

All four stakeholder types have different perceptions of "success."

In this book, I purposely avoid the temptation to make recommendations on such issues as:

- which asset classes or asset class segments are the most appropriate for a pension or investment fund;

- whether internal management is more attractive than external management;

- whether active management is more cost-effective than passive/ index approaches, given the expected value-added results;

- which investment style provides the best risk/reward trade-off over the longer term; and,

- which investment vehicles are the most appropriate.

These decisions depend on the nature of the plan sponsor, the plan design, and the goals and objectives of the pension or investment fund. The decisions also depend on the risk tolerance and appetite, and the beliefs and experiences of the investment committee members, the board, or any other governing body that has the authorities and responsibilities for the ongoing administration (either directly or in-directly) of the investment funds. Each investment fund has its own specific characteristics, and these decisions should be custom designed for each fund to reflect those characteristics.

For plan sponsors, one challenge lies in attempting to calculate the overall financial cost of overseeing, administering, and managing monies for fund participants. One of the responsibilities of the plan sponsor is to ensure that the rewards are justified given the costs of managing the investment program.

One final observation is that investment committee members are not expected to be experts on all things related to investing fund activities. That would be virtually impossible. However, investment committee members *are* expected to have sufficient in-depth knowledge and education to select the resources and professional expertise, internally and externally, to achieve the goals and objectives established for the investment funds entrusted into their care.

Accepting the role of an investment committee member has particular responsibilities. Beneficiaries depend on the investment committee's actions and decisions. This book is designed to assist investment committee members in navigating through the required governance process.

Every pension and investment fund has an objective that drives the decisions of the investment committee members. Their overall responsibility is to act prudently. This role cannot be overstated: their decisions have significant consequences for the fund beneficiaries. As a trustee, fiduciary, or administrator, the investment committee members have an obligation to gather the experience needed to fulfill their role.

In my 50-plus years within the investment field, I have worked as an investment officer within the investment department of a financial institution; as the chief investment strategist within a plan sponsor organization—where all pension monies were managed internally; as an investment planning consultant within a large, global investment planning consulting organization; and, finally, as managing director and chief operating officer within an independent investment management firm. Over my career I have attended and participated in well over 1,500 investment committee meetings sponsored by government bodies, corporate organizations, operating and endowment funds, financial institutions, foundations, and charitable organizations. As well, I have interviewed, evaluated, ranked and continuously monitored over 150 investment management organizations for our consulting clients. This book highlights my experiences and observations from attending many investment committee meetings and interacting with investment committee members. The examples and stories I discuss come from these various investment committee meetings. I believe all the information I have provided in this book to be factual. When using examples or making observations, I will state the role I was in at the time.

This book was written during the COVID-19 pandemic. The pandemic has proven to be a life-altering event for the vast majority of people around the world. The longer-term effects on the world's various economies and capital markets could prove to be staggering. The repercussions of the pandemic have the potential to significantly affect the risk/reward relationship of the various asset classes selected within the investment management structure. For the members of investment committees, the challenges presented by the pandemic are numerous. Committee members must have in place a business continuity program that ensures that processes are in place for the continuous administration, monitoring, and evaluation of the investment fund assets. The past century has rarely produced a set of challenges as great as those we are witnessing today.

An investment committee member is one of the most important roles within any plan sponsor or other organization that has a fiduciary responsible for administering, overseeing, and managing other people's money. This book is designed to assist committee members in understanding their obligation to plan beneficiaries and how to achieve success when implementing the designated investment program.

CHAPTER ONE

THE ROLE OF THE PLAN SPONSOR

Building the Foundation

Just a thought:

It seems like my education days were wasted.
I took math, geometry, algebra, trigonometry,
and calculus in high school and university;
however, I have yet had to solve for x.

INTRODUCTION

One of the primary responsibilities of the plan sponsor in its legal role as administrator of fund assets is to create a foundation outlining the mission, beliefs, processes, and procedures for the effective and efficient implementation of an investment program. Typically, responsibility for implementing this investment program is delegated to an executive- or management-level investment committee. However, the plan sponsor is responsible for setting the goals and objectives of the investment program, based on the plan type and its characteristics.

Key issues the plan sponsor must address include:

- within the mission statement, determining the appropriate risk tolerance and appetite of the investment fund in light of the plan's liabilities;

- outlining specific investment beliefs (e.g., active management vs. passive/index tracking);

- determining the requirements and roles of all service providers responsible for administering and managing fund activities;
- creating an investment committee with qualified members to implement investment policy;
- setting investment goals and objectives;
- formulating longer-term asset mix policy;
- selecting and approving money managers and establishing their mandates and performance standards;
- creating various ongoing maintenance policies;
- monitoring and evaluating ongoing fund activities against stated goals and objectives to learn from past results and maximize the odds of future success;
- designing effective reporting processes and formats to communicate transparently and clearly with the governing body and the plan members; and,
- most importantly, operating in the best interests of the plan beneficiaries.

The importance of the role of the plan sponsor cannot be emphasized enough. The decisions made at this level can significantly add to or subtract from pension and investment assets. On the one hand, if the plan sponsor makes the wrong decisions (or fails to make the decisions it should), these decisions could erode the investment fund's longer-term rate of return by knocking off a percentage or two per annum in total performance. This could increase the long-term cost of delivering a targeted level of retirement benefits by up to 25%, reduce the amounts of benefits to the same degree, or result in greater risk than the fund and risk bearer(s) may be able to tolerate when the worst happens.

The outcome can have three major consequences:

1. plan beneficiaries are negatively affected, as future benefits may have to be lower than promised, targeted, or hoped for;

2. the plan sponsor is less able to attract and motivate key personnel; and,

3. for a corporate plan sponsor, the overall business or activity can be placed at a competitive disadvantage if significant capital has to be channeled to the pension or investment fund rather than being reinvested back into the main lines of business.

On the other hand, in fulfilling its fiduciary role, the plan sponsor can and should create an appropriate risk/reward balance, formulate a suitable asset mix policy, design an effective investment management structure, and hire well-qualified personnel for the various internal and external functions. In so doing, the plan sponsor can significantly enhance returns over time and establish the necessary communication processes to provide security and comfort to all plan beneficiaries so that their retirement dreams can be achieved.

The plan sponsor must recognize and accept that its circumstances are unique, which means that it must customize its own set of beliefs, principles, values, objectives, preferences, standards, etc. to satisfy its specific requirements.

ROLES AND FUNCTIONS OF THE PLAN SPONSOR

Before an investment committee can be established, the plan sponsor must first address certain responsibilities, as shown in Figure 1.1 below:

FIGURE 1.1: PLAN SPONSOR RESPONSIBILITIES

STRUCTURE	MISSION	RISK/ RETURN	POLICIES	INVESTMENT COMMITTEE	OVERSIGHT
Roles	Beliefs	Appetite	Ethics/conduct	Roles	Content
	Goals	Opportunity	Conflicts	Experience	Format
	Roles		Confidentiality	Membership	Frequency
			Social		Communication

STRUCTURE

The conceptual structure below outlines an organizational hierarchy designed to oversee, administer, manage, monitor, and evaluate the activities of a typical pension plan and investment fund, as Figure 1.2 shows:

FIGURE 1.2: PLAN SPONSOR STRUCTURE

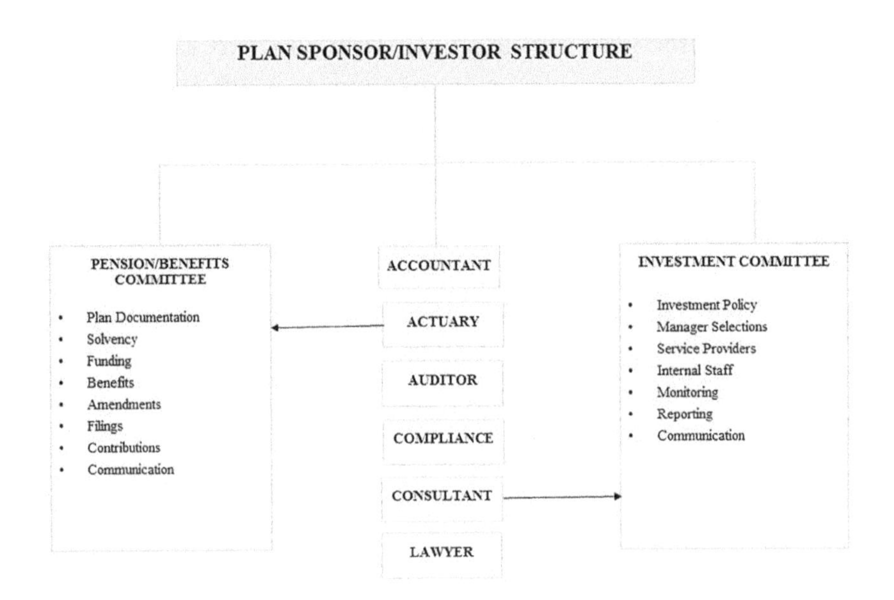

As shown in Figure 1.2 above, the various professional resources available and necessary to the plan sponsor comprise:

- the *accountant* monitors the activities of the pension plan or fund as they relate to a corporation's financial statements;
- the *actuary* establishes the plan structure and design, and prepares ongoing actuarial valuations of the plan's funded status;
- the *auditor* tracks the fund activities;
- the *compliance officer* monitors ongoing investment committee activities and provides checks and balances on the system as a whole;
- the *pension consultant* or *investment planning consultant* provides ongoing advice on all aspects of the pension plan and investment funds; and,
- the *lawyer* provides legal advice when necessary.

MISSION

The first issue to be addressed is to formulate the overall *mission* of the fund—which is critical for developing a framework to achieve the desired goals and objectives. There are both fundamental differences across, and lesser nuances within, individual pension plans and investment funds. These differences will likely vary across plans based on their perceived risks, funding sources, and time horizons. The plan sponsor must recognize these key aspects and custom design the mission to meet all obligations. There is no cookie-cutter approach here. The mission outlines the plan sponsor's envisioned outcome that provides safety, predictability, stability, and comfort to all plan beneficiaries. The mission should result in a clear understanding of the risks that the plan sponsors are willing to accept, as well as the achievable return objectives needed to deliver the promised or targeted benefits at an acceptable level of contributions.

Corporate plan sponsors and government-sponsored plans must determine the plan characteristics that drive the specific objectives for the investment of the fund assets. These characteristics typically include:

- the plan type (e.g., defined benefit, target benefit, defined contribution, or hybrid);
- benefits promised or targeted;
- the plan's longer-term durability, intimately tied to the plan sponsor;
- demographics of the plan members—notably, the split between active members and retirees;
- events that could cause a significant plan adjustment or even discontinuance;
- the plan's funding—normal contributions and sources, how adverse experience may affect contribution levels and sources, and the capacity for increased contributions if needed;
- the predictability (usually fairly high) of cash flows moving in and out of the pension or investment fund;
- requirements for liquidity and cash generation to pay benefits;
- status (e.g., non-taxable) of pensions and some investment funds; and,
- the sensitivity of plan finances to inflation through its impact on benefit payments—both those already earned and benefits to be earned in the future.

In setting the goals and objectives, sensitivity to inflation is a particularly important influence to consider. Inflation erodes wealth over time. For plan sustainability, an adjustment for anticipated inflation must be incorporated into the longer-term required rate of return.

Plan Sponsor Beliefs

To provide investment committee members with a foundation for how plan assets should be administered and managed, it is necessary to outline the *beliefs* of the plan sponsor and, therefore, for members who must form consensus around these beliefs. Stated beliefs, derived from reliable evidence and rational arguments beyond general "motherhood-type" statements, provide a visible and viable basis for the investment committee's decision-making processes.

When setting out these investment beliefs, three main issues should be considered:

1. the longer-term *timeframe* of a pension plan must provide higher confidence that future investment returns will reflect the historical features of the trade-off between return and risk;

2. *asset mix policy* should be the main determinant of both return and risk—both ex-post and ex-ante; and,

3. appropriate *diversification* should be considered the only "free lunch" owing to its role of reducing risk in pursuing required returns or, on the other side of the coin, of enhancing expected returns at a tolerable level of risk.

As well, the plan sponsor must determine whether to have the investment funds managed internally or externally—or some balance of the two. The decision is typically made based on two main factors: 1) the size of the assets within the fund; and 2) the business nature of the plan sponsor. Economies of scale may enable mega funds to internally manage some or all of these investment functions at significantly lower costs, yet with comparable success to that of external providers. Plan sponsors that themselves specialize in delivering money management services may elect to leverage their operational skills by managing their funds internally.

Besides better pricing, some of the commonly recognized advantages of internally managed funds are:

- greater control over the investment strategy, investment selection, and implementation;
- greater risk-management control;
- a more in-depth understanding of the decision-making process, as it can be custom designed to meet the specific goals and objectives of the fund;
- full-time attention to singular or smaller numbers of portfolios;
- potentially, lower trading costs; and,
- more effective operating controls, monitoring, and evaluation criteria.

Meanwhile, the advantages of having the fund assets externally managed include:

- greater access to more expert resources to execute and support the decision-making process;
- the ability to provide for greater diversification by asset class, investment approach, and investment style; and,
- greater flexibility to add or eliminate money managers from the investment management structure.

Fund size usually dominates the decision whether to have all or some of the investable assets of the fund managed internally.

Finally, plan sponsors must constantly revisit and assure themselves, as best possible, that there is no disconnect between their beliefs and emerging investment realities, or between beliefs and fund activities.

Goals and Objectives

The pension plan sponsor is expected to have a good working knowledge of the longer-term rate of return required for the fund to fulfill the promises made to all plan beneficiaries. Plan sponsors are given a "target" return as a base to start from—the minimum actuarial rate of return assumed necessary to ensure that the funds to pay all future obligations are available when needed. However, there is a range of uncertainty around this target, as it depends on many assumptions. The plan sponsor needs to understand, from the actuary, the key assumptions being made and how sensitive the required target return is to these assumptions. However, the investment return objective is to exceed this actuarial going-concern valuation rate.

Figure 1.3 below shows why setting goals and objectives is difficult:

FIGURE 1.3: THE PENSION FUND DILEMMA

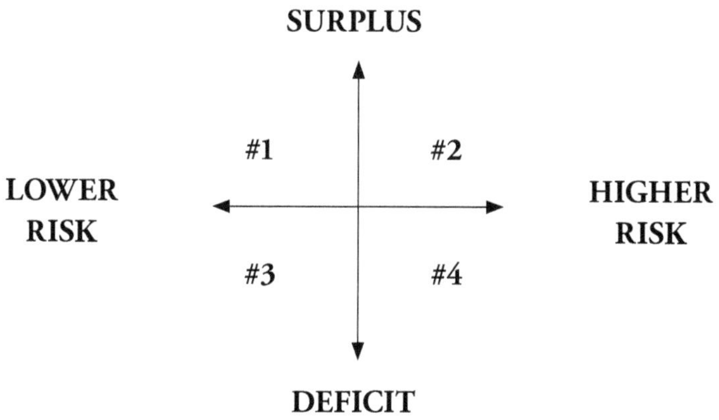

SURPLUS

#1 #2

LOWER RISK HIGHER RISK

#3 #4

DEFICIT

In the top half of Figure 1.3 above, the plan sponsor has been fortunate enough, over time, to have built up a fund surplus of, for example, 10% (i.e., the plan is 110% funded).

- With Option #1, the plan sponsor has decided to "protect" the *surplus* by reducing the overall risk of the fund (e.g., allocating more monies to less volatile asset classes or shortening the average term to maturity structure within the fixed-income segment). The asset mix shifts to assets with more predictable and stable return patterns.

- With Option #2, the plan sponsor decides to stay the course, and asset mix policy remains the same. The plan sponsor may even increase risk (still within an acceptable level) with the view that the margin of safety for benefits delivery has increased.

In the lower half of Figure 1.3, the fund is in a deficit position. Again, there are two options.

- With Option #3, the plan sponsor is concerned that the *deficit* may worsen—which may require a cash infusion. As a result, the plan sponsor decides to take a more defensive or conservative stance and moves monies into more stable and predictable asset classes, hoping the deficit does not worsen.

- With Option #4, the plan sponsor decides that the only way to reduce or eliminate the deficit is to take on more risk (e.g., increasing equity-type assets of the fund), hoping to earn higher future returns.

It is best not to spend too much time trying to figure out this conundrum as, unfortunately, there is no right answer—and, perhaps, no wrong answer. In my experience, deciding which option to implement is, generally, determined by the attitudes, emotions, and experiences of the investment committee members and plan sponsor, their perceptions of where the components of the capital market are today, and their outlook for the foreseeable future (usually, over the next 6 to 12 months). Decisions are not necessarily based on the fundamentals of the plan or what is best for the plan beneficiaries. Unfortunately, this means that the focus on the long-term nature of the fund (policy-driven) is replaced with short-term, often reactionary, emotional market timing considerations (strategy-driven).

In my experience as a plan sponsor, money manager, and investment planning consultant, I have found little to no correlation or link between the current funded status of a pension plan and the asset mix structure within the fund—whereas, in principle, there certainly should be, on a basis agreed upon before the funding status changes.

As indicated, investment policy is all too often driven by the plan sponsor's belief about where we are in the current capital market cycle. However, investment policy should be changed only under extreme circumstances (either the characteristics of the plan have changed or the components of the capital market have become highly overvalued or undervalued). Furthermore, even if the components have shifted substantially, the decision to temporarily depart from policy should be more deliberate and *strategic*, with both a stated time horizon to revisit the change and signposts to be monitored along the way. It seems that plan sponsors tend to be more concerned with avoiding short-term perceptions of failure than with achieving longer-term success. In other words, avoiding risk is a risk in itself.

In summary, the overall goals and objectives of the plan sponsor are:

- to maximize the security of the fund assets for all plan beneficiaries;
- to maximize the longer-term total return of the pension and investment assets without undue risk—and assess what "undue" means;
- to lower the short-term volatility of funding, contributions, and, possibly, corporate net profits; and,
- to do all this with a longer-term focus on controlling overall costs.

Roles (Authorities and Responsibilities)

There can be four main decision levels within the plan sponsor governance structure designed to oversee, administer, and manage pension and investment fund assets. And each of the four levels may have various types of authorities and responsibilities assigned to them.

Board and Board Sub-committee: The board's main task is *formulating investment policy*. Given that plan sponsors have the fiduciary responsibility to oversee and administer large pools of investment funds, the board (or governing body) must set the framework for the investment program. The board must first address the set of beliefs needed to deliver the desired results for the investment assets. These beliefs will include capital market-specific beliefs and organizational beliefs. Capital market-specific beliefs will include which asset classes will provide the best risk/reward trade-off, whereas organizational beliefs will focus more on whether assets should be managed internally or externally.

The issues to be addressed in creating an investment policy statement include:

- determining the overall risk tolerance and appetite of the fund;
- designing a functional asset mix policy;
- determining which asset classes should be included, the desired target mix for each asset class, and the tolerance ranges that would trigger a rebalancing;
- setting the performance standards for the fund as a whole, for each asset class segment, and for the money managers; and,
- creating a policy on social investing.

The board is also responsible in its role as a fiduciary for:

- setting the parameters for selecting service providers (e.g., actuary, investment planning consultant, money managers, and the custodian);
- establishing the required reporting processes and procedures to effectively monitor ongoing investment activities to fulfill its role as a fiduciary; and,

- delegating authorities and responsibilities to the chief investment officer (if in place), the investment committee, and internal staff.

Chief Investment Officer (CIO): The CIO's main responsible is to *implement investment policy*. As a result, the CIO must formulate and recommend overall investment strategy related to the investment program.

The CIO's responsibilities include:

- recommending an asset mix to achieve the desired goals and objectives of the fund;
- setting the parameters for the investment management structure;
- determining the performance standards for the internal and external investment managers;
- creating the processes and procedures needed to monitor and evaluate policies and service provider activities; and,
- monitoring and evaluating the effectiveness of the investment committee and internal staff.

Internal Investment Committee: The investment committee has the overall responsibility of *implementing investment strategy*.

The responsibilities of the investment committee may include:

- monitoring and evaluating asset mix policy;
- recommending an effective investment management structure;
- recommending various policies (e.g., broker selection and commission allocation, pricing, security lending, proxy voting, currency exposure, and soft-dollar usage);

- recommending money managers, as well as recommending termination when appropriate;

- monitoring and evaluating all external service providers; and,

- monitoring and evaluating the overall effectiveness of the internal investment staff.

The responsibility of the investment committee will be addressed in more detail in Chapter Two.

Internal Investment Staff: The investment staff is, basically, responsible for monitoring the day-to-day activities related to implementing the *investment program* as a whole and the ongoing activities of the service providers.

The responsibilities of the internal staff may include:

- monitoring and evaluating the money managers;

- recommending policies;

- recommending performance standards and tracking the money manager performance;

- providing education, information, and data to the investment committee;

- tracking pension and investment industry trends that might either increase the returns of the fund, reduce the risks of the fund, or reduce the costs within the investment program (e.g., tracking the costs of administering the fund assets against the set budget); and,

- ensuring that all issues are in compliance.

As indicated earlier in this chapter, with the four decision levels described above, two factors come into play: the first is *size*. The first two levels shown above (i.e., board and CIO functions) are generally associated with plan sponsors with very large pools of money to invest. For the average pension and investment fund, the process typically begins with the internal investment committee—as delegated by the plan sponsor or similar overseeing body. This committee typically has three to five members, one of whom may spend 100% (or at least the majority) of their time on investment matters—with, perhaps, one or more investment support staff. The pension and investment funds of the plan sponsors with smaller pools of money are just as important to these organizations as they are to the very large funds that can afford more resources; however, the smaller funds are not likely to have the same depth of experience within their internal staff. As a result, the overall responsibilities of administering pension and investment assets might be relegated to the investment committee level.

The second factor is *investment experience.* Designating responsibilities works only if the CIO, investment committee members, and internal staff have the necessary investment knowledge (or access to this knowledge) to administer and manage the investment program effectively and efficiently. Plan sponsors should not delegate activities to a level that is incapable of effectively hiring external service providers or monitoring, evaluating, and reporting on the various activities required to fulfill their fiduciary duties.

It is appropriate that the plan sponsor retains some authorities and delegates only specific authorities and responsibilities to the chief investment officer and internal investment committee. Ultimately, the board or other senior governing body has to accept fiduciary responsibility for all eventualities for the major sums of fund assets held in trust for others, including poor investment outcomes.

RISK AND RETURN TRADE-OFF

One of the most difficult tasks for any plan sponsor to address is in determining the "optimum" balance between risk and reward (or, as close to optimal as possible). What makes this difficult is that both risk levels and return objectives change over time. The good news is that the *risk* levels of the various asset classes are more predictable and stable through time than returns are—and, when risk levels do change over time, they do so very gradually. The relative *volatilities* of the various asset classes have been fairly consistent over the past 40 or so years. This trend alone enables (even dictates) a risk-based foundation for developing investment policy.

Furthermore, the *correlations* between asset classes are also somewhat predictable and fairly constant over time. When correlations do drift, they generally move closer together in down markets, which, unfortunately, results in lower diversification benefits when most needed.

Return expectations are more difficult to predict—specifically, over shorter-term time horizons. However, given that most pension funds and some investment funds are generally long-term in nature and have relatively low liquidity requirements, longer-term return expectations for both traditional equity-oriented asset classes and fixed-income investments allow for fairly reasonable educated "guesses"—although there are distinct 10- to 20-year "eras" or "regimes" in history in which returns have deviated significantly from historical averages.

When predicting asset class returns, there are both risks and uncertainties associated with the outcomes. The components of the capital market can deviate from their long-term averages for a significant period of time; therefore, one should distinguish between "risks" (which have somewhat reasonable models to predict potential frequency and magnitude) and "uncertainties" (which can be identified but for which no reliable models exist). Dealing with uncertainties requires building, testing, and weighing alternative scenarios for the future, rather than relying on only statistical models and history.

Risk Appetite

To state the obvious, and as has been observed repeatedly, pretty much all investors are risk averse (i.e., one unit of potential downside carries more weight than one unit of potential upside). Determining the *degree* of this risk aversion is what's required. What makes this difficult is coming up with an agreed-upon definition of "relative risk." Risk has different meanings for each party associated with the investment fund:

- the *plan sponsor* might define risk as not achieving the goals and objectives of the fund—which could result in a cash infusion or reduced benefits;

- the *investment planning consultant or actuary* might define risk from a capital market perspective and focus on the balance between equity-type securities and fixed-income investments; and,

- the *money manager* may define overall risk as deviating too far from the designated performance benchmark or the performance of peers (and, of course, being fired).

So, risk has different meanings to different parties—and the *degree of risk* to each party may change over the timeframe given.

Determining risk tolerance and risk appetite provides the basis from which plan sponsors can formulate investment beliefs. There can be a significant difference between *risk appetite* and *risk perception*. Risk appetite is typically based on facts and measures, and is considered over a longer-term time horizon—a more rational approach than risk perception. Risk perception is typically based on human emotions, attitudes, and experiences, and it depends more on short-term events than risk appetite does. On a rational basis, tolerance and appetite for risk should be the focus—determining the willingness and ability to take on risk. However, as the field of behavior finance has repeatedly shown, few, if any of us, would be considered rational.

In my experience, risk aversion has dominated the risk/reward equation. The focus by most plan sponsors has been more on the risk side of the equation than on the reward side. This is not surprising, given that returns are harder to predict, and that regulatory agencies and funding rules tend to emphasize the importance of reducing overall risk. However, I personally believe that pension and investment funds have adopted an overly conservative role—which has resulted in far lower returns on fund assets than could or should have been the case. I attribute this caution mainly to the inexperience of investment committee members. A lack of knowledge and experience in any field typically results in a more conservative approach to decision-making, especially in the pension and investment industries—the unknown is scary.

Return Potential

In theory and logic, the higher the levels of risk, the greater the return potential—which is the reason that the assets of the vast number of pension and investment funds are predominately in ownership-type investments. The stock market returns for both the U.S. and Canada for the past 90-plus years have been about 10% per annum (in nominal terms). Since 1950, there has been only one time period when the U.S. stock market had three negative return years in a row (2000, 2001, and 2002), and only one other period when the markets had two negative calendar years back-to-back (1973 and 1974).

Given the historical risk/reward trade-off, betting against equities over the long run would have been costly.

POLICIES

At a minimum, there are basically four main policies that must be adopted by the plan sponsor:

- a *code of conduct* or *ethics policy*—outlining appropriate behavior for the CIO, all investment committee members, and internal staff;

- a *conflict of interest policy*—ensuring that the investment committee members operate in the best interests of all fund beneficiaries and that their decisions are free from biases and self-interest;

- a *confidentiality policy*—ensuring that what should be kept confidential stays that way; and,

- a *social responsibility policy*—outlining beliefs related to social responsibility issues, including attitudes toward climate change.

All investment committee members should sign these policies to show that they accept their role as a fiduciary, trustee, and/or administrator.

Refer to Appendix 1 for a sample policy covering conduct, ethics, and confidentiality.

ESTABLISHING THE INVESTMENT COMMITTEE

The plan sponsor must now determine what types of authorities and responsibilities it wishes to delegate to the members of the internal investment committee. They may include:

- determining the role of the investment committee, what experience is required, and committee membership;
- outlining the formal reporting formats, processes, and procedures;
- determining the frequency of contact; and,
- assigning accountability to the committee as a whole.

Roles, Experiences, and Skills

Some tightly organized committees identify a specific role for some or all committee members, in addition to their general overall responsibilities. Clearly, a chairperson must be identified, but also, certain members may be identified to lead, for example:

1. monitoring, evaluating, and meeting with the various service providers;
2. tracking investment performance, and providing risk analysis and outlook; and,
3. covering operational and communication matters.

As mentioned earlier in this chapter, very large pension and investment funds may have two investment committee levels: external (board level) and internal (management level).

In my experience working with external investment committees, I have found three main tendencies: first, in many cases, external investment committee members tend to *lack the education and experience* needed to carry out their fiduciary duties. These members may be brilliant in their own areas of expertise, and may be well educated and well meaning; however, there may be a significant disconnect between their various fields and the knowledge required to understand the investment business—particularly that of pension funds. Without this knowledge, it is difficult, if not impossible, for committee members to effectively formulate investment policy and set the standards for all service providers linked to the pension and investment fund activities. The second tendency of external investment committees is the *lack of time and commitment* allocated to their governance role (e.g., establishing, overseeing, administering, monitoring, analyzing, evaluating, and communicating the ongoing activities of the pension/investment funds).

And third, committee members, in most cases, tended to be *short-term thinkers*—reacting more emotionally and quickly to recent events. With limited knowledge of the mechanics of the components of the global capital market, they tend to be more like market timers—frequently wanting to move from one asset class to another, or from one manager to another, based on recent short-term results (i.e., acting more like the average buyer and seller of mutual funds).

For medium- to smaller-sized pension and investment funds, the internal committee is typically the only committee. Its members are selected or elected from inside the organization (either corporate, government sponsored, or multi-employer). However, the weakness of internal investment committees is the same as that of external committees—a lack of investment experience. Mid-size and larger pension and investment funds typically have a chief investment officer and/or a team of three to five specialists who are fully dedicated to managing the investment fund's activities. As the assets administered under the plan sponsor get smaller, the number of people responsible for pension activities declines to the point at which, within smaller organizations, there may be only one or two people who spend less than 100% of their time on the pension or investment program. Unfortunately, there is no surefire approach to filling positions on investment committees due to the dependence on the size of assets of the funds entrusted to the investment committee's safekeeping.

The saying "a little knowledge is a dangerous thing" was, perhaps, never more meaningful than to an investment committee. Committee members, over time, may forget that their role is that of an administrator and begin to edge toward making decisions that fit more within the investment realm. They begin to think of themselves as market strategists. They begin to second-guess the investment decisions of the money managers, yet they have no process of measuring the success of their own actions. Investing is always easy—when critiquing the actions of others in hindsight.

Selecting Investment Committee Members

In theory, selecting investment committee members should be no different from the process that the plan sponsor would use to hire personnel in any other division within the organization, or any other important functions of the plan sponsor. Criteria for the necessary attributes of ideal candidates should be determined by the plan sponsor in advance. This is all part of the due-diligence governance process. However, in reality, investment committee members seem to be selected based on their position outside the organization, their status within the organization, or their length of service within the organization. Their educational background, relevant experience within the investment field, or knowledge and competency to fulfill their role as fiduciaries and trustees are seldom considered. The primary management function of the plan sponsor is to administer the investment activities of the fund, which should be given the same amount of attention as any other major division within the organization—and in some mature organizations with large funds, maybe, even more.

Membership

Investment committees should be made up of people with various levels of education, backgrounds, and experiences (at least, that is how it *should* be). In an investment committee, the most important position is that of the chairperson. This person *must* have investment knowledge, be able to run meetings effectively, understand the importance of excellent implementation, be able to bring in expertise from the outside when required, and be able to establish effective reporting, monitoring, and evaluation formats and processes from all relevant service providers. I believe that the person in this position should be an investment professional with the Chartered Financial Analyst designation who has no conflicts of interest (i.e., not still working within an investment management firm, or an investment consulting or actuarial organization), or should have at least 20 years of experience within the pension or money management fields.

Some other factors to consider in committee membership:

- *Size*: During my time in a money management organization and as an investment planning consultant, I worked with and reported to investment committees that had from 3 to 10 or more members. Based on this experience, I consider the optimal size of an investment committee to be between three and five members—depending on the experience of the members. The more members with investment experience, the lower the number of members required; however, there should be no fewer than three members. Three members can provide for some diversity of thought and allow for the minimum checks and balances.

- *Term limits*: I believe that the board-level committee, or any other senior investment committee that has external committee members, should have term limits—albeit with an exceptional option for renewal. The time can vary between three and five years. This results in new members bringing in new ideas, experiences, knowledge, and judgment. In addition, as committee members work together for a few years, members know what expertise they lack and can, hopefully, fill in any gaps by adding new members.

It might be difficult for mid- to smaller-sized funds to have term limits—as there might not be significantly relevant experience within the plan sponsor organization. And, without exception, inclusive diversity certainly improves committee behavior and performance.

- *Investment planning consultant*: Each investment committee should have an outside consultant who can assist in formulating policy, researching and recommending investment managers, providing measurement dynamics on the fund and money managers, providing insight into trends in the pension and investment environments, and proactively bringing new ideas to the investment committee. Beyond providing consulting services, the consultant should have no conflicts of interest (e.g., selling investment management services or investment management products). Unfortunately, this has become rarer within the consulting field as more and more consulting firms move into providing money management services. As well, like external committee members, consultants should have term limits of three to five years until a review date. If there are two investment committee levels, each committee should have its own consultant relationship.

- *Understanding*: Global investment markets are quite sophisticated, with new approaches, products, and investment vehicles being introduced monthly. It is very difficult for even dedicated investment professionals to keep up with this speed of change. As committee members have different levels of knowledge, it is necessary for *all* committee members to be onside with decisions taken—no one should be left behind. Committee members should not defer to other members who seem to understand (it might be too late when members find out that their committee colleagues were also unsure of the decisions being made). In most committees, there always seems to be one person who dominates meetings (and not necessarily the person who possesses the most knowledge or experience, or has the best education or best ideas, but, usually, the one who pounds the table the hardest and longest). The chairperson must ensure that all members have the opportunity to express their views and have access to all information required to bring everyone up to speed.

- *Overlap*: If there are two separate and distinct investment committees, there should be at least one person who is a member of both committees to ensure ongoing continuity and accurate communication back and forth.

- *Over-management*: It is very difficult for investment committee members not to second-guess their investment managers' decisions in hindsight. Thus, beyond ascertaining what happened, and why, members should not interfere in the decision-making process of the money managers selected.

- *Advice*: If you ask for outside advice and it makes good sense (e.g., it is sound and has potential to reduce overall risk materially, increase overall returns, reduce overall costs, or improve governance and accountabilities), don't ignore it completely just because the advice might be uncomfortable, unfamiliar, or outside the bounds of common practice. Use the advice to narrow the gap between beliefs, policy, strategy, and implementation.

- *Affiliations*: It is necessary to know whether any investment committee members are affiliated with companies or entities that are suppliers of products or services to investment funds, or are board members of any public companies that may result in conflicting interests with their fiduciary responsibilities. I have found that some plan sponsors are hesitant to ask senior board members to provide this detailed information for fear of offending the member. It is better to be up-front than to fail to detect a conflict of interest. It is part of the fiduciary responsibility of committee members. This should be addressed in the conflict of interest policy.

In summary, it is admittedly difficult to find the right complement of members for an investment committee. At least some members should have in-depth knowledge of investment markets and be able to make judgment calls about what will positively affect the activities of the fund in the longer-term best interests of beneficiaries. There are many courses and training seminars to make investment committee members more effective in their fiduciary role, and, hopefully, to allow committee members (and plan beneficiaries) to sleep well at night—the ultimate test of prudence. Investment committees should be established and designed by thought, rather than by default. Members should not be shy about seeking out external experts to assist in administering and managing fund assets.

OVERSIGHT

The last but by no means least important responsibility of the plan sponsor is to ensure that the overall investment program is effectively monitored for success. The plan sponsor should regularly review information and analysis that track and measure all the activities of the investment fund to ensure that its goals and objectives can be achieved. The plan sponsor should delegate the responsibility for gathering pertinent information to the investment committee or internal staff, along with any other requirements to fulfill its fiduciary and administrative responsibilities. Within the oversight responsibility, there are three important functions as outlined below.

Reporting Content and Format

Investment committee members must be able to effectively evaluate the various activities of the investment fund. This is where accountability comes into play.

A regular update report should include the following:

- compliance with the investment guidelines;
- an update on the asset mix position;

- recent and historical performance at the asset mix level for the total fund against the "normal" or "neutral" policy, and for each asset class and asset class segment;
- portfolio characteristics;
- individual money manager performance and attribution against the performance standards they were given; and,
- updates on any changes within the money management organizations.

This update should be provided at least annually, not necessarily quarterly, and certainly not monthly.

The format and length of the update should be designed to provide all relevant information and analysis as efficiently and effectively as possible. As most plan sponsors have time constraints, the format should result in the plan sponsor spending no more than 30 minutes being briefed on all pertinent house-keeping activities—leaving room in meetings to focus on more pressing issues. Appendices should be used routinely for more in-depth information. The investment committee and internal staff should be doing all the heavy lifting to prepare the updates accordingly.

Meeting Frequency

The frequency of meetings is at the discretion of the plan sponsor, in coordination with the organization's other activities. With effective information updates from the investment committee and internal staff, the number of meetings can be kept to a minimum—in most cases, semi-annual meetings should be sufficient—if the plan sponsor trusts committee members and staff to do professionally what they have been delegated. Special meetings should be held to address specific topics (e.g., issues out of compliance with investment guidelines, whether any asset classes are approaching their tolerance ranges, or changes within a money management organization or other service provider that may be of concern).

The investment industry thrives on being able to measure anything that moves. Ours is an industry of data overkill—and, I believe, with the main intent of confusing and bewildering plan sponsors. Just because something can be measured does not mean it should be measured. Data are not necessarily information, and information is not necessarily knowledge or insight. The plan sponsor can get bogged down with information overload. Committee members should measure what is important, and with that, distinguish between signal and noise (i.e., changes within the range of normal variation)—in other words, the committee shouldn't get distracted by what isn't.

Thus, effective oversight completes the loop from the planning stage through the operation/implementation stage to overall maintenance and control. It is all part of the due-diligence process.

Communication with Beneficiaries

One of the responsibilities of the investment committee is providing effective and timely communication to existing beneficiaries of the plan. The information shared should provide comfort to all beneficiaries that their funds are in capable hands. However, in practice, communication with plan beneficiaries often seems to receive the least amount of time and energy spent, and seems to be a relatively low priority for the plan sponsor. Beneficiaries, typically, do not have the investment expertise to understand the importance that capital market returns have in creating or securing wealth for their retirement years. The plan sponsor has the responsibility to both inform and educate—whether within a defined-benefit plan or a defined-contribution plan.

In summary, the role of the plan sponsor is to create an investment program for the sole benefit of the plan's beneficiaries. Plan sponsors must act in a fiduciary function to ensure that the administration, management, and implementation of the investment program is free from biases and conflicts of interest.

Plan sponsors must:

- outline their specific beliefs;
- determine the goals and objectives needed to deliver on the promises made to beneficiaries;
- understand the risk tolerance and appetite at the total fund level;
- set the framework for asset mix policy; and,
- create oversight processes and procedures as a check that the various components of the investment program are delivering as expected.

One of the primary responsibilities of the plan sponsor is to set up an investment committee to implement, execute, monitor, and evaluate all activities related to the ongoing investment of all plan assets. In so doing, the plan sponsor must determine the roles, authorities, and responsibilities of the members of the internal investment committee. The highest priority is to ensure that the committee members have the investment knowledge, experience, and skills needed to implement the investment program effectively and efficiently.

I have purposely attempted to distinguish the roles and responsibilities of the plan sponsor from those of the investment committee. Chapter Two addresses the roles and responsibilities of the investment committee.

CHAPTER TWO

THE ROLE OF THE INVESTMENT COMMITTEE

The King of Committees

Just a thought:

Just think, without time, everything
we know would happen all at once.

INTRODUCTION

In any treatise on the topic of investment committees, interested parties would be inundated with the following terms: prudence, due diligence, care, skill, transparency, duty, loyalty, and, more rarely, common sense. While all of these terms are important, they are used sparingly throughout this book in favor of the fundamental concept underpinning them—that is, prudence. It dominates everything else. If investment committee members get prudence right, everything will fall into place. Prudence is not judged by investment results alone, many of which are beyond the full control of the investment committee—rather, it is judged by the process by how the investment committee members made their decisions and conducted their oversight of the fund assets. The prime responsibility of the investment committee is to look after the interests of the plan beneficiaries. Of course, that is the easy part. The hard part is *how* to do this. Investment committee members are responsible for determining the road map and are the driving force that spans the period from the plan design stage to fulfilling the obligations undertaken by the plan sponsor.

I *won't* say that the majority of investment committees are dysfunctional; however, I also *can't* say that the majority are functional. My observations are not because the members of most investment committees are not the brightest, are not highly educated, do not have the best intentions, do not prioritize the best interests of the plan beneficiaries, or do not have impressive experience or credentials—although experience is too often insufficiently related to the fiduciary investment field. They typically have these qualities. However, the four main detriments to a well-functioning investment committee are a lack of:

1. relevant background and experience in dealing with the complex nature of the financial markets and their interactions with the finances and security of the plan;

2. understanding regarding the multiplicity of investment products and vehicles available;

3. in-depth knowledge of the various service providers that operate within the pension and investment environments and their motivations; and,

4. time to successfully, effectively, and efficiently design and implement investment policy.

As a result, there is often a significant disconnect between policy, strategy, and implementation. To improve the performance of the investment committee, any gaps must be closed.

As stated above, the *processes* that the investment committee implements to formulate decisions that outline members' beliefs and principles, determine and select the appropriate internal and external resources, and set up effective reporting and control procedures are as important as the *decisions* themselves—for which there may be no right or wrong answer. Members may be "judged" more on the process, which they can control, than on the end results, which they might not be able to control. Members can also be appropriately assessed on the totality of their considerations—particularly for defined or target benefit pension funds. The characteristics are unique to each plan (e.g., based on the split between active members and retirees, duration of these liabilities, discount rate used, and inflation sensitivity).

The investment committee is typically made up of members who have volunteered, or been chosen or elected by the plan sponsor and/or the plan participants. The members have a general fiduciary duty under common law to act for and in the best interests of *all* the plan beneficiaries. When acting as fiduciaries for fund assets, investment committee members must place beneficiaries' interests first, and they must be able to distinguish between that role and any other role they may have to represent the interests of the plan sponsor (the "settlor" function) and act accordingly. The plan sponsor delegates responsibilities and authorities to investment committee members based on what is laid out in the plan document itself and what is directed and required by trustee and pension benefits acts of the various jurisdictions—as well as other regulatory agencies.

Bottom line: Members of an investment committee have the sole duty to protect the interests of the plan beneficiaries. As a result, the plan sponsor has to set in place the parameters for the investment committee to ensure that it acts in the best interests of all beneficiaries.

FIDUCIARY ROLE OF INVESTMENT COMMITTEES

One of the most important requirements of the plan sponsor is to fully understand its role as a fiduciary, trustee, and/or administrator. Fulfilling the duties of an effective fiduciary requires acting in a "prudent" manner. The various regulatory bodies associate "prudence" in the administration of pension and investment funds as providing for appropriate *diversification* and establishing risk-management parameters. However, while appropriate diversification and risk-control procedures are important in managing any fund, they are by no means the sole considerations.

The Employment Retirement Income Security Act (ERISA) defines the term fiduciary as any person who:

- Exercises any discretionary authority or discretionary control regarding management of the plan, or exercises any authority or control (discretionary or otherwise) regarding management or disposition of its assets; or

- Renders investment advice regarding plan assets for a fee or other compensation, direct or indirect, or has any authority or responsibility to do so; or

- Has any discretionary authority or discretionary responsibility in the administration of such plan.

CFA Institute recommends a code of conduct for pension trustees (as addressed in its *Pension Trustee Code of Conduct and Guidance for Compliance* publication). According to CFA Institute, pension trustees should:

- Act in good faith and in the best interest of the plan participants and beneficiaries.

- Act with prudence and reasonable care.

- Act with skill, competence, and diligence.

- Maintain independence and objectivity by, among other actions, avoiding conflicts of interest, refraining from self-dealing, and refusing any gift that could reasonably be expected to affect their loyalty.

- Abide by all applicable laws, rules, and regulations, including the terms of the plan documents.

- Deal fairly, objectively, and impartially with all participants and beneficiaries.

- Take actions that are consistent with the established mission of the plan and the policies that support that mission.

- Review on a regular basis the efficiency and effectiveness of the plan's success in meeting its goals, including assessing the performance and actions of plan service providers, such as investment managers, consultants, and actuaries.

- Maintain confidentiality of plan, participant, and beneficiary information.

- Communicate with participants, beneficiaries, and supervisory authority in a timely, accurate, and transparent manner.

In some cases, investment committee members act as trustees for the investment funds under their authority. A trustee is, generally, a person that holds or administers property or assets for the benefit of a third party—having discretionary authority, responsibility, and control over those assets.

A trustee must:

- understand the terms, mission and objectives of the property/assets/funds entrusted into its care;

- ensure that the funds are prudently invested, avoiding any conflicts of interest that might provide a bias between any personal interests and those of the individual beneficiaries; and,

- have overall knowledge regarding the legislation and regulations that relate to the assets or funds being invested.

The Prudent Expert Act, a regulatory measure contained within ERISA, requires a fiduciary to act "with the care, skill, prudence and diligence under circumstances then prevailing that a prudent man acting in a like capacity and *familiar with such matters* would in the conduct of an enterprise of a like character with like aims..." (Italics added.)

In summary, for pension and investment funds, the fiduciary is responsible for:

- developing policy;

- determining risk assessment and appetite;

- ensuring appropriate diversification throughout the investment program;
- appointing experts; and,
- creating oversight management and operating procedures that ensure that goals and objectives are achieved in a cost-effective way.

ROLES AND RESPONSIBILITIES

Figure 2.1 below summarizes the different responsibilities of the investment committee members. Each responsibility is addressed in the sections thereafter.

FIGURE 2.1: ROLES AND FUNCTIONS OF THE INVESTMENT COMMITTEE

INVESTMENT POLICY	ASSET MIX POLICY	INVESTMENT STRUCTURE	POLICIES	OVERSIGHT	MEETING AGENDA
Beliefs	Asset classes Weights Rebalancing	Active/ Passive Mandate Vehicles	Soft dollars Proxy Trade Lending Valuation	Activity Assessment Evaluation Updates	Compliance Content Minute Chairperson Membership Binders

Typically, the investment committee has three main functions:

1. to design and implement an investment program that can be expected to *earn an acceptable return* on the monies entrusted in its care;
2. to achieve this return objective within *an acceptable risk tolerance/ acceptance*; and,
3. to create and execute this targeted risk/return trade-off at *a reasonable cost.*

Given the outline of the responsibilities shown in Figure 2.1 above, the most important document established by the plan sponsor, or as delegated to the investment committee, is the investment policy statement.

CREATING AN INVESTMENT POLICY STATEMENT

The statement of investment policy and procedures is the starting point for the investment committee. This statement is a required formal document designed to outline all policies, processes, and procedures to guide and provide oversight of all investment activities within an investment program. This statement must:

- incorporate all requirements of the applicable regulations and legislation;
- be reviewed and either confirmed or modified regularly (e.g., annually);
- be custom designed to reflect the plan type, the characteristics of the plan, and the nature of the plan sponsor; and,
- reflect the investment beliefs of the plan sponsor as represented by the investment committee.

This statement should be prepared in coordination with all relevant parties: the plan sponsor represented by the investment committee, the actuary and/or investment planning consultant, and the money managers. All parties have a vested interest in achieving the goals and objectives of the fund. As a result, all parties should commit to this formal document in order to deliver the desired results.

The investment policy statement should also include:

- the fundamental purpose of the investment fund, as related to the plan;
- investment objectives and time horizon;

- key elements of the risk/reward appetite and trade-off;
- the rationale for asset class diversification and selection (and rejection);
- asset mix weightings, tolerance ranges, and rebalancing;
- the investment management structure to implement the above points;
- the selection criteria of the money managers (either internal or external); and,
- processes and procedures for monitoring, evaluating, and assessing the various investment activities of all internal resources and external service providers.

In addition, the investment policy statement itself, or an accompanying operational document, should outline the specific roles and responsibilities of all service providers, highlight any liquidity requirements, determine accountability and reporting procedures, outline performance standards, and formulate processes and formats to monitor and evaluate all pertinent, measurable investment activities effectively.

Investment policy statements should also provide in-depth detail as required—in particular, they should effectively outline what courses of action should be taken if certain events occur. Doing so would reduce the chance for emotional reactions based on recent events as much as possible.

Beliefs

One of the more important tasks of the investment committee members is to agree upon a common set of beliefs as they relate to the various segments of the capital market. The following capital market beliefs should be addressed: first, investment committee members need to decide whether they believe that markets are *efficient*—or not. If specific asset classes or asset class segments are perceived to be within a relatively efficient market, then the focus should be on seeking out passive/index-matching approaches within these markets that will mirror the asset class, or asset class segment, at the lowest fee. Active management is a viable alternative if investment committee members believe that: a) some markets are inefficient and can be exploited by active management to provide a value-added return, within an acceptable risk tolerance, while more than compensating for the cost and risk of active management; and b) that valued-added managers can be identified in advance with sufficient confidence. If choosing active management, the investment committee must also recognize that costs matter—costs are certain, whereas the value added is uncertain.

A second market-related belief is the importance of *time*. The pension or investment fund is usually (but not always) considered to have a longer-term time horizon (i.e., disbursements from the fund will continue many years in the future); in that case, depending on the resilience of required contributions in downturns, short-term volatility of fund results might not be a major concern. From a return perspective, the odds significantly favor ownership-type assets the longer the perceived time horizon. Studies have stated that an additional long-term net return of 1% per annum may well reduce long-term funding costs by 15–25% in an open plan or for a defined-contribution plan member, and by 10–15% in a closed plan or for a retiree living on a pool of assets.

Another market-related belief is the concept of *mean reversion*. One of the few truisms within the capital market is that returns tend to revert back to their normal trend line over time. However, there are two caveats here: the first is determining what the "normal" trend line is, which too can change with the era or regime, and the second is that the direction of the expected reversion is much more evident than its timing.

In addition, there is the belief that *higher risk can be compensated for by higher returns*—for sound economic reasons. The focus here is to determine the extent of: a) the shorter-term market price risk that the fund and its risk-bearers are willing to accept; and b) the greater uncertainty of longer-term dollar downside. Note, again, the difference here between "risk" and "uncertainty."

Refer to Appendix 2 for an outline of an investment policy and procedures statement.

FORMULATING AN ASSET MIX POLICY

Determining which asset classes and sub-asset classes to include within the investment fund, and the weighting of these asset classes, have, by far, the greatest impact on the overall return of the fund and on the level of risk (both short-term volatility and long-term range of possible outcomes). As a result, the asset mix policy is the most important, ongoing single decision that the investment committee will make.

Asset Class Selection

The first decision is to determine which asset classes to include (or exclude) within the asset mix policy. Asset classes are divided into two broad categories: *ownership-type assets* (e.g., common stocks and real estate) and *fixed-income assets* (e.g., preferred stocks, bonds, and mortgages). Most of the asset classes and asset class segments that make up the asset mix have indexes that provide the plan sponsor with historical asset class returns and volatility levels, and also, as a result, correlations between one asset class and another. With this information, asset classes can be blended for appropriate diversification within the asset mix structure. Generally, the lower the correlation between the asset classes, the better the fit within the structure (i.e., the less similar the asset class return patterns and the securities within the asset classes, the greater the diversification benefit).

Without going into minute detail on the many asset classes and asset class segments available to the plan sponsor, Table 2.1 below highlights the primary asset classes used most frequently for pension and investment funds:

TABLE 2.1: PRIMARY ASSET CLASSES

OWNERSHIP-TYPE	FIXED-INCOME
• Stocks: Domestic - Large cap - Small cap • Stocks: Non-domestic - Global - Regional - Emerging markets • Real estate • Alternatives - Infrastructure - Private equity - Private debt - Hedge funds - Commodities	• Cash/short-term securities • Mortgages • Preferred stocks • Bonds - Domestic government - Foreign government - Corporate - Investment grade - High yield • Bonds - Short-term - Mid-term - Long-term

Asset Class Weighting

Investment committee members should provide reasons why certain asset classes were selected (e.g., based on the return objective and risk appetite of the fund as a whole, as outlined by the plan sponsor), as well as why certain asset classes were not selected (perhaps due to excessive complexity or unacceptable risk levels). The second step is to determine the "policy" (also referred to as "neutral," "normal," or "target") mix weighting allocated to each asset class and sub-asset class, as well as a tolerance range (desired upper and lower limits) for each. A sample asset class structure for a North American pension or investment fund is shown in Table 2.2 below.

TABLE 2.2: SAMPLE ASSET CLASS WEIGHTING

ASSET CLASS	POLICY PORTFOLIO (%)	TOLERANCE RANGE (%)
• Equities (40%)		+/– 10
– Domestic stock	15	
– Non-domestic stock	20	
– Emerging markets	5	(Max 10)
• Real estate (10%)	10	+/– 3
• Alternatives (10%)	10	+/– 5
– Infrastructure		
– Hedge funds		
– Private equity		
• Fixed-income (40%)		+/– 10
– Domestic	25	
– Non-domestic	10	
– High yield	5	(Max 10)
	100	

NOTES:

1. Up to 15% of the domestic stock portfolio may be held in small/ mid-cap stocks.

2. Cash is held within the various portfolio segments.

3. Up to 25% of the real estate portfolio may be held in non-domestic markets.

4. The return-seeking component (equities, real estate, and alternatives) should not exceed 70% of the total fund, based on market value.

5. Within the fixed-income segment, the domestic and non-domestic sectors have a minimum quality rating of investment grade—with no more than 50% in corporates.

Rebalancing

As every asset class experiences different return patterns over time, the asset class weights will drift and begin to diverge from the policy weights. According to theory (and confirmed by history), equity-type investments tend to outperform fixed-income investments over longer periods of time, as they have the potential to provide capital appreciation, and, hopefully, an increasing income stream. Over certain market cycles, it could take a significant amount of time for equity-type investments to outperform fixed-income assets, although they consistently have over the last 100 years. As a result, the weighting of equity-type investments within the asset class structure should, over time, begin to increase, and, as a result, the overall targeted risk in the fund may also increase. However, in the short term, it is not uncommon for equity investments to rise or fall in value by 20% or more in any given year. As an asset class approaches its upper or lower tolerance range, a rebalancing mechanism must come into play—if the overall intended diversification and risk levels are to be maintained.

There are three main approaches to rebalancing:

1. *Time-driven*: The asset mix can be adjusted back to the policy portfolio triggered on a fixed-period basis (e.g., rebalanced at each quarter-end, at calendar year-end, or every three years). One major disadvantage of time-driven rebalancing is the transactional costs of making frequent or inefficiently small moves between asset classes, sub-asset classes and, perhaps, money managers. While conceptually simple, time-driven rebalancing is arbitrary with little investment rationale.

2. *Policy-driven*: This occurs only when the weighting of an asset class, or asset class segment, reaches or approaches its tolerance range. In Table 2.2 above, if the overall equity weight were to reach 70%, it would trigger an automatic rebalancing. With this trigger, there are two main options: a) rebalance all asset classes back to the policy weight; or b) trim the equity weight back to some predetermined weight (e.g., halfway between the existing weight and the policy weight). Then, either adjust all other asset classes by some predetermined formula, or, to better reduce transaction costs, successively adjust the asset classes that are furthest away from the policy weight until the intended equity weight is reached.

3. *Cash-flow management*: Most pension and investment funds tend to have positive cash flows entering the fund throughout the year—through both contributions and income from securities held. There are three options within this approach: a) allocate cash flow (in or out) on the basis of the policy portfolio—with cash flow distributed to each asset class and sub-asset class according to the policy mix (e.g., if alternatives had a 10% weighting within an overall policy portfolio, 10% of the cash flow would be allocated to the alternative component); b) allocate to each asset class and sub-asset class segment based on the current *market value* of the asset classes within the portfolio (e.g., if the alternative weighting increased to 12% of the total fund, then 12% of the cash flow would be directed to alternatives); or c) judiciously allocate each cash flow toward reducing any gaps between current and policy weightings. The cash-flow management approach carries the lowest transaction costs (one side only). However, it might not be possible to maintain an asset class or asset class segment within all its tolerance ranges, in which case it may be necessary to resort to policy-driven rebalancing.

Rebalancing is, basically, a contrarian approach to investing, as the better-performing asset classes are rebalanced to the lesser-performing asset classes—all centered on the concept of mean reversion. Rebalancing maintains the desired risk profile.

I have found that the best rebalancing approach is to let the assets in the portfolio drift until an asset class has reached the outer limit of its tolerance range—and then rebalance back to the policy weight. It might take a decade or so for asset drift to actually trigger a rebalancing (depending on how wide the tolerance ranges are)—keeping the transaction costs from rebalancing to a minimum. However, a substantial variation in the risk and diversification profile has to be accepted, which may be regretted if markets turn fast and substantially when offside. I also prefer to allocate cash flows based on the *market value* weights of the various asset classes and asset class segments. The equity component holds stocks, real estate, and alternatives as investments; it may be diversified by geographic region and investment style complements, and is broadly diversified by sector and security selection. It is unlikely that the overall risk exposure, at the total fund level, would increase significantly if the equity weighting moved from 60% to 70%.

Several studies in recent decades have stated that the asset mix decision can represent as much as 90–95% of both the volatility and return of the total performance of an investment fund over longer periods of time. Without carefully defining "asset mix decision" (notably, vs. an alternative), this broad assertion is a major exaggeration about total fund or individual portfolio returns and should be questioned. These studies appear to be well researched and documented; however, as each investment fund has its own asset mix (consisting of various asset classes) with different weights that have been custom designed for that specific plan and its risk tolerance and appetite, it does not help to provide an average of a few arbitrary plans—as no pension plan may have that average. Furthermore, if, say, 90% of the return of an investment fund were due to the asset mix decision, then the remaining 10% must come from other sources. The only sources that could have a major positive influence on the residual 10% are the investment selection and timing decisions of the plan sponsor and the positive contributions of the money managers. The plan sponsor could make a minute contribution by setting up a security lending program or a commission recapture program—however, neither of these activities is likely to move the needle. An active money manager could add some value to the overall return by achieving value-added results above their designated benchmark/index. However, from the money management side, value could also be lost against the benchmarks assigned after including all active management expenses (management fees and transaction costs). In addition, any study on the topic of return allocation between the asset mix allocation and active management is always time sensitive and sample centric. What works in one time period might not work in another. Even though many later studies have brought more clarity to how different decisions contribute to the returns, the original over-simplified or unqualified assertion remains a popular belief.

Another factor to consider is the all-in costs of administering and managing the plan sponsor's fund assets. These costs clearly offset some, or even all, of the value added from the money managers. As a result, the asset mix returns in an absolute sense indeed represent something close to 100% of the total fund return—however, this is simply the returns on the markets themselves, not the contribution of the decision to choose one particular mix versus another.

Bottom line: The asset mix decision over the longer term may represent close to 100% of the total fund return and, basically, all of the risk.

Refer to Appendices 3 and 4 for a history of stock market returns for the U.S. and Canadian markets on an annual basis for the past 90-plus years.

INVESTMENT MANAGEMENT STRUCTURE

In the design of an investment management structure, many issues have to be considered—such as active management versus passive/index-matching approaches, diversification, investment management styles and approaches, and investment vehicles.

Active Management versus Passive Approach

The most important decision at the investment management level is based on the belief of the investment committee regarding the efficiencies of the various capital market components. If members of the committee believe that an asset class is inefficient and, therefore, can be exploited to add value-added results to the fund over the cost associated with managing these asset classes, then active management should be considered for at least part of the fund, if not all of it. However, for active management to meet the test of fiduciary prudence, the members must also believe that they, or their advisors, have the *expertise and skill* to select money managers that have the potential to outperform the market net of all costs. If committee members believe that markets are very efficient and active judgments cannot offset the cost of active management, then low-cost passive approaches are available for many asset classes and asset class segments. However, it's not an either/or decision: most decisions on how actively to manage pension and investment fund assets result in a mix of active and passive management.

Mandate

The number of opportunities for constructing a well-diversified stock portfolio for the plan sponsor has expanded significantly over the past three decades. Beyond the asset mix decision at the total fund level, stock portfolios can be further diversified by:

- *Geographic allocation:* Stock selection from among the various regions of the world has the greatest impact on overall returns at the stock portfolio level.

- *Investment styles*: There are basically three primary investment management styles used in creating stock portfolios: growth, value, and market-oriented. Simply, *growth* managers focus primarily on company dynamics (e.g., companies that are dominant in their field and individual company prospects) and growth-focused metrics, with an emphasis on asset growth, capital growth, earnings growth, and return on capital. These managers seek out *companies* that are expected to grow faster than other companies within their sector and faster than the economy as a whole. *Value* managers mainly focus on market-related value-focused metrics with an emphasis on price (e.g., relatively low price/earnings ratios, relatively high dividend yields, and relatively low price/book ratios). These managers tend to seek out stocks that sell below what they perceive to be their true "intrinsic" value. *Market-oriented* managers (sometimes called "core managers," "blend managers," "growth-at-a-reasonable-price managers," or "sector rotators") are fairly well diversified and their portfolios tend to look more like the broad stock market indexes over time.

As much as consultants would like plan sponsors to believe that growth managers and value managers are at the opposite ends of the investment-style spectrum and, therefore, are excellent and pure complements to each other, they are not—they simply hold two broadly different beliefs about how to construct portfolios. If they were indeed opposites, there would be few or no overlapping stocks in the portfolios of each style—yet there are. A relatively large percentage of the securities contained within a broad stock market index cannot be classified as either growth or value. It should also be noted that investment style is not a "skill." Rather, it is an inherent belief of the money manager in where and how their focus is best directed.

There are two distinguishing characteristics of the two main investment styles. First, growth managers focus on the "e"-side of the price/earnings multiple (the statistical measure used when determining the relative value of a company's share price against another on a comparable basis) and are therefore more interested in *company* dynamics as indicated above. Value managers are more focused on the "p"-side of the price/earnings multiple, placing more emphasis on market-related *stock* statistics. Second, value managers are big believers in "mean reversion," whereas growth managers, not so much. Value managers are always hoping for mean reversion, whereas growth managers hope it never happens.

- *Capitalization*: Many money managers operate in a certain stratum of the stock market, given their beliefs about where they most successfully find attractive stocks with their investment management skills. Over longer periods of time, small- and mid-cap stocks have outperformed large-cap stocks—which is consistent with their higher risk profile. The active manager's rationale here is that smaller companies are under-researched, and, therefore, skillful money managers focusing on this area of the marketplace believe they can find great unrealized value.

- *Investment approach*: The two main approaches to portfolio construction of both stock and bond portfolios are a *top–down* approach (e.g., focusing on macro-economic variables and trends in political and social environments) and a *bottom–up* approach (which emphasizes the attributes of individual securities). As well, some money managers with a large research staff may focus on a *qualitative approach* to security selection, while other organizations focus more on a *quantitative approach*—using systems and models designed to construct portfolios.

There are two main reasons for this trend toward greater diversification within investment funds: first, regulatory authorities around the world have encouraged plan sponsors, investors, and money managers to place greater emphasis on "prudence" in their portfolio construction process—where prudence is primarily defined by appropriate diversification. Second, cash flows from pension funds, other investment-type funds, and individuals have increased so significantly over the past four decades that it has become virtually impossible for the medium to larger money management firms to build concentrated portfolios.

Investment styles, approaches, and options within the fixed-income area have also expanded significantly since the 1990s, as they have for the stock component. As domestic stock portfolios can be augmented with non-domestic stocks, plan sponsors can augment their domestic fixed-income portfolios with non-domestic bonds. As for sectors, the main focus is the allocation between government/quasi-government securities and corporate issues. Generally, to be considered for inclusion by a plan sponsor, a corporate issue is typically classified as being "investment-grade" (typically, rated BBB and above by the various bond rating agencies) or "high yield" (below investment-grade). For the main investment styles, bond managers can be *sector/quality rotators* (moving between different areas of the fixed-income marketplace—from sector to sector or quality level to quality level) or *interest-rate anticipators* (moving up and down the yield curve based on the relative value between short-term securities, mid-term securities, and longer-term bonds). Over time, high-yield securities often act a lot like stocks during certain market cycles, as their yield spreads over government bonds, and their market prices are therefore more dependent on economic events and corporate-specific attributes than on the trend or level of interest rates. Over the past 20 to 30 years, high-yield securities have performed well against other fixed-income securities—even given their higher risk level.

Investment Vehicles

There are two main investment vehicles to consider after determining the asset classes, investment approaches, and investment styles: *commingled or pooled* funds and *segregated or separate* portfolios. A commingled fund is unitized and managed for multiple clients—combining their assets within one investment vehicle. Commingled funds enable money managers to attract clients who have smaller pension and investment funds on a cost-effective basis—for example, the portfolio is easier to monitor, there is less paperwork, and compliance is less onerous. The plan sponsor benefits from economies of scale, as its assets are combined with those of other clients for less costly trade execution. On the other side, a segregated portfolio is managed exclusively for the benefit of an individual client within a specific mandate. The difference between these vehicles is twofold: first, the segregated portfolio is more attractive to plan sponsors with specific investment guidelines and constraints that would make their portfolio unique (e.g., prohibiting investments in tobacco, firearms, or gambling stocks) or with specific financial requests (e.g., security lending programs or soft-dollar/directed commission arrangements); and second, the fees may be slightly higher for a commingled fund than for a segregated portfolio. This is one of the many anomalies within the investment field: a money management organization often charges more to "mass produce" a product (commingled fund) than to "custom design" a portfolio (segregated) with an almost identical investment mandate.

For the vast majority of clients, a commingled vehicle is simple and acceptable—except where fund-specific guidelines differ from the guidelines associated with the commingled fund. Commingled funds are typically promoted by money management firms as their "model" portfolio for a given asset class. As a result, segregated accounts with the same mandate as a commingled fund should track the performance of the commingled fund fairly closely—or vice versa. However, within a commingled fund, there could be some hidden charges (e.g., transaction fees, custodial fees, and audit fees). The money manager can provide the cost of these internal charges. As well, in some cases, a commingled fund might not be appropriate owing to tax considerations.

INVESTMENT MANAGEMENT AGREEMENT

Created by the plan sponsor for the money manager, the investment management agreement is a document that provides detailed instructions for how the money manager should invest funds, and sets out the financial terms for doing so.

In many cases, plan sponsors combine the investment policy statement with the investment management agreement. It is preferable that these be two distinct documents. The *investment policy statement* covers many broad topics, all of which are in the domain of the plan sponsor, whereas the *investment management agreement* outlines requirements that are specific to each individual mandate given to the money manager (e.g., sector and security weight maximums or highlighting prohibited investments).

As a result, the investment management agreement is custom designed specifically for each individual money manager and investment mandate. This agreement provides a framework and strategic guide for the manager in carrying out its investment management responsibilities. The agreement should begin with a brief overview of the plan itself and the applicable beliefs of the plan sponsor.

The following items should be clearly addressed in the investment management agreement:

1. the desired goals and objectives for the managed portfolio;

2. liquidity requirements (if any);

3. risk tolerance (both absolute and relative to the performance benchmark and value-added target);

4. investment guidelines and constraints;

5. quality levels;

6. performance standards (with a designated benchmark and value-added target);

7. time horizon for performance measurement;

8. manager discretion;

9. reporting (by whom, format, and frequency);

10. fees (structure and payment process);

11. data requirements; and,

12. terms for and causes of termination.

With respect to manager termination, the investment management agreement should outline the circumstances that may trigger termination (e.g., failing to comply with the written mandate; unacceptable changes within the portfolio, organization, or the investment management team; changes in ownership; changes in the decision-making process or investment style; and substantially underperforming the desired performance targets over the stated time horizon without acceptable explanations). Furthermore, the agreement should include a notice period for when monies must be returned in the event of termination. The standard period is 30 days; however, if the infraction is severe enough and the portfolio is perceived to be at risk, then the monies should be withdrawn immediately.

Within the investment management agreement, there should be a set of performance standards for each money manager and investment mandate. Performance standards, as they relate to benchmarks, have three components: the first is the *timeframe* over which the performance of the portfolio will be measured—the most common timeframe being rolling periods of four years. The second component is selecting the appropriate *benchmark* for each of the investment mandates. The benchmark is typically a passive bogey or market index that closely represents the investment universe for the portfolio the money manager is managing. The benchmark establishes the base for measuring the manager against the plan sponsor's expectations. In addition, later results will shed light on whether the plan sponsor was correct to select active management. The third component is the *value-added target* above the designated benchmark. It should bridge the gap between the expectations of the plan sponsor and the manager's capabilities to achieve clear alignment and, subsequently, to justify the decision on active management. If the manager cannot deliver sufficient risk-adjusted results above the benchmark after active fees, the plan sponsor may be paying too much for what might have been passive/ index returns (at best).

Regarding below-expected performance, it is good practice to agree with the manager in advance what the normal range of performance variation around the benchmark will be. The investment committee members and the money manager should also agree on the tolerance band for a major shortfall below the targeted rate of return, and the point at which the manager can expect to be terminated without further ado.

Comparisons of performance results fall into three main categories: absolute, relative, and comparative.

1. An *absolute* approach employs one set standard (e.g., a certain percent above the inflation rate over a longer-term time horizon, or the actuarial valuation return rate required for plan sustainability).

2. A *relative* measurement approach employs one or more specific benchmarks (usually against a market-specific index).

3. A *comparative* approach presents the manager's performance against that of a peer-group sample to compare portfolio performance against like managers and/or like funds.

Refer to Appendix 5 for an outline of an investment management agreement.

POLICIES

The investment committee should create, at a minmimum, five main policies:

1. *Soft-dollar/Directed commission policy*: Sets out how commission dollars generated through trades in the portfolio are to be allocated and how much discretion the manager has. "Soft dollars" refers to the amount of the commissions paid to a brokerage firm on a transaction over and above the actual cost of executing the trade. Refer to Chapter Seven for more details on soft dollars.

2. *Proxy voting policy*: Indicates to the money manager and the custodian how proxies are to be voted, and by whom.

3. *Trade allocation policy*: Requires "best execution" when directing transactions through the brokerage community.

4. *Security lending policy*: Outlines the procedures to be taken when securities are lent from the portfolio.

5. *Valuation policy*: Sets out an unbiased process for placing a fair value on non-marketable securities when no pricing data are available through the public market.

In addition to these five policies, plan sponsors may have additional policies that are unique to their own organization (e.g., governance standards, socially responsible or "ethics" investing, the purchasing of company stock if a public company, and climate change initiatives).

Refer to Appendix 6 for a sample policy for trade and brokerage allocation and to Appendix 7 for a sample proxy voting policy.

OVERSIGHT AND COMPLIANCE

One of the main functions of an investment committee is to develop the effective and efficient framework needed to monitor, analyze, and evaluate the various activities of money managers and other service providers within the investment program—both individually and collectively. The investment committee is responsible for gathering the pertinent information to ensure that the investment program is on track to deliver the desired goals and objectives.

The investment committee must review four necessary reports and updates on a predetermined schedule:

1. *Compliance Report*: Regularly tracking the allocation among the various asset classes and money managers, the guidelines and constraints given to each individual manager, and quality levels.

2. *Portfolio Composition and Activity Report*: Tracking various pre-established, relevant portfolio characteristics to ensure that each management organization is staying true to its investment style and approach.

3. *Performance Evaluation Report*: Covers how well each manager is meeting its performance standards, as well as the performance patterns.

4. *Money Management Organization Update*: A constant review of changes withing money management firms, including personnel, investment style or process, monies flowing in and out of the mandate chosen, and ownership.

Day-to-day oversight is generally the responsibility of the plan sponsor's internal investment staff, although they may require substantial assistance from the money managers and investment planning consultant(s).

Designated internal staff must ensure that the investment committee members are kept up-to-date that everything is working as intended within the investment program—to reduce and eliminate any surprises.

INVESTMENT COMMITTEE MEETING AGENDA

Investment committee members must consistently address many issues and topics in a well-organized way. The issues and topics are likely to, or at least should, vary from meeting to meeting. As such, the length of time for each meeting should vary depending on the topics on the agenda. However, in reality, meetings typically have set start and end times, with a quarterly meeting usually lasting two or three hours, regardless of the topics on the agenda. The agenda topics should determine the meeting length—one meeting could last only an hour, whereas another could and should take up the whole day.

For effective investment committee meetings, the following elements are important:

- *Compliance*: The first item that should be reviewed is compliance. The discussion is usually a brief but necessary form of due diligence. It should ensure that every activity related to the investment fund that is being monitored and evaluated is in compliance with the stated goals, objectives, and guidelines. Internal staff should maintain a checklist of items that can be measured (e.g., asset mix targets and ranges, investment guidelines and constraints given to investment managers, quality levels, and performance standards). Compliance should be at the top of each agenda. Fortunately, this is also an easy item—if the scorecard reads "in compliance," it can simply become a filed report with no discussion. However, if any line item is out of compliance, or close to becoming so, enough time should be allocated to agree on how to remedy the specific issue(s) through whatever steps are necessary.

- *Content:* Internal staff should prepare the agenda and deliver it to investment committee members, as well as to external managers and advisors who may be attending or contributing, well in advance of the meeting. An adequate amount of time to review all accompanying reports to be addressed at the next meeting is two to three weeks (not two to three days). The most important items should be first on the agenda.

- *Time allocation*: As indicated above, the original time allocation should be a function of the topics on the agenda and the complexity of the issues to be addressed. I have found that the vast majority of investment committee meetings I have attended could have been completed in about half the time, if issues and topics were better defined and had stricter time limits. Often, committee members are distracted by too many "little shiny objects," resulting in committee members moving off topic. If any issues or topics arise that are not on the agenda (provided they are not urgent matters, and the committee members agree that they are important enough for further discussion), then the chairperson should place the issue on the agenda for a future meeting, whether regular or ad hoc. Unfortunately, most meetings tend to be focused on process rather than driven by content.

- *Money manager interviews*: Investment committee members seem to enjoy meetings with money managers. Unfortunately, while often entertaining or even expertly insightful about what is happening in the capital markets, in most meetings with money managers, much of the content provides very little useful information on the historical performance, ongoing portfolio positioning, or realistic prospects in the management of pension and investment funds. I know that it is a kind of unwritten rule that manager review sessions must happen—and I don't disagree that they should; however, it is up to the committee members to make these meetings effective and useful. In my role as an investment planning consultant, I have lost count of the number of money manager review sessions I have attended with our clients. Some meetings would last a full day with presentations from up to six managers. At the end of the day, the clients' eyes would glaze over and they had very little recall of any of the money manager sessions.

Internal staff can help address this problem by preparing a report in a format that highlights all measurable activities of the money manager. This "report card" should have at least a five-year history (or as far back as the relationship with the manager goes) of all the relevant information (e.g., any lawsuits or pending lawsuits; changes in ownership; changes in investment personnel; client additions to or departures from the mandate; changes in total assets under management; new products or services; performance against standards). The importance of a five-year history (or longer if possible) is to determine if there are trends (drifts) developing within the portfolio that might negatively impact the expected performance of the assets or change the risk profile of the portfolio entrusted into the manager's care.

Next, the pertinent portfolio characteristics and significant transactions (best and worst) should be described in a way that provides evidence (or otherwise) of how the actual portfolio aligns with the investment beliefs, values, and decision-making processes that were expected when the money manager was hired.

Not all managers need to be seen quarterly, semi-annually, or even annually. If all is unfolding as hoped for, it might not be necessary to waste the time of the investment committee members, or to take time away from the manager in managing the portfolio.

I strongly believe that there are too many unnecessary manager review meetings. If things are going well, let your manager be. In addition, the frequency of meetings should depend on the specific mandate (e.g., real estate managers do not need to be seen quarterly—their portfolios do not change that often) and the comfort level between the committee and the manager.

- *Internal investment staff*: Every now and then there should be a review of the quality of work being undertaken by the internal, investment-related staff. Basically, the evaluation should assess whether staff members are proactive in keeping themselves and investment committee members up-to-date with trends within the pension and investment world. The investment committee should consider the necessity of staff members taking courses. Most importantly, have committee members effectively communicated what they expect from staff personnel, and are they comfortable with what they are getting? Effective communication is required here.

- *Minutes*: Document everything. Minutes should record who was present at each meeting, what issues and topics were discussed, and the approval of previous minutes. Provide as much detail as possible so members who did not attend the meeting could feel as if they were actually there. The minutes should be accurate, clear, and concise. If votes were taken, record who was in favor and who was not. In addition, items for the next meeting should be discussed, agreed upon, and recorded with the necessary detail. This type of discipline saves second-guessing the past. A recording secretary should be appointed.

- *Chairperson*: None of the suggestions above work well without an effective chairperson. An "effective" chairperson is defined as having sufficient in-depth knowledge of the investment community and their processes, being open to all opinions, having no conflicts of interest, and being able to effectively and efficiently manage the ebb and flow of meetings. Most importantly, the chairperson should have the time to manage the process effectively. There should be a written job profile for this position and documented explanations of why and how the chairperson was appointed or elected. The chairperson should create a culture that permits committee members to freely express their thoughts and concerns.

- *Ongoing membership:* There should be a process in place to remove a member from the investment committee for specific reasons (e.g., conflicts of interest, being disruptive to the process, lack of participation, and missing meetings).

- *Outside consultant*: It is useful for an investment planning consultant to attend every meeting, mainly as an observer and translator, to provide clarification on certain issues and topics, interpret what money managers are saying or trying to say, and to provide continuity. The consultant can also provide knowledgeable opinions and take a position rather than just sitting on the fence.

- *The binder*: A major benefit of complete and accurate minutes is when new investment committee members replace existing members. A binder containing the decisions made at the investment committee level over the past few years allows new members to be brought up-to-date fairly quickly on what has been decided in the past and why. The binder saves time in meetings, as other committee members do not have to explain why the fund is tilted toward equities, why a particular money manager was hired, etc. Committee members are constantly changing. The background information in the binder ensures that new committee members can be brought up to speed and can participate in these meetings from day one.

In summary, the role of the investment committee is to administer the investments and investment-related activities of a pension and investment fund for the sole benefit of the participants and their beneficiaries. Nothing could be simpler, in principle; however, it is no easy task to do well in practice. The investment committee members are charged with the responsibility to understand, monitor, analyze, evaluate, and act in the best interest of all beneficiaries. The number of members on an investment committee is typically determined by the size of the pension or investment fund under management. Too few members might not achieve the diversity and experience necessary, while too many could prove unruly.

Legislation and regulations are constantly changing in both the pension area and the investment field. Committee members must be sufficiently familiar with the plan documents, trust agreements, and governing legislation.

As indicated at the beginning of this chapter, the success of pension and investment funds depends on the experience, knowledge, and skills of the investment committee members. I believe that the investment committee is the most important committee within most plan sponsor organizations. To ensure the investment program's success, the investment committee members should have an ongoing review process in place that monitors and evaluates the decisions they make, perhaps using the internal audit group. This process would, hopefully, encourage the plan sponsor to place the most appropriate people possible on the committee. There is nothing like self-analysis to direct and keep the focus where it belongs.

In closing this chapter, I quote from CFA Institute from their *Pension Trustee Code of Conduct and Guidance for Compliance* publication: it is critical for pension plans to be "overseen by a strong, well-functioning **governing body** in accordance with fundamental ethical principles of honesty, integrity, independence, fairness, openness, and competence." (Emphasis in original.) Does this sound like your investment committee?

Refer to Appendix 8 for an outline of an investment committee mandate statement.

CHAPTER THREE

PERFORMANCE INHIBITORS

The Seven Headwinds

Just a thought:

Over the years, I have found that if there is
a 50/50 chance of me being right or wrong,
I will be wrong at least 90% of the time.

INTRODUCTION

The investment management community lives and dies by the performance results of the portfolios and funds managed by investment professions. Very few industries have the degree of oversight and scrutiny that is placed on all aspects of the activities that go into delivering investment performance (from investment policy at the plan sponsor level through to implementation at the investment manager level). It is virtually the only industry in which the participants know on a day-to-day (or even minute-by-minute) basis whether their portfolios are achieving the return objectives of the plan sponsors.

Many factors have the potential to impact overall performance results materially—long before the monies have even been placed with the investment managers. The decisions made at the policy level can have a greater negative impact on fund performance than can the underperformance of an investment manager. However, it appears that investment committee members spend around 90% of their time tracking money manager performance, and firing/hiring managers when things go wrong, leaving little time to evaluate the bigger picture.

As a result, there are several potential performance inhibitors that could have a significant detrimental impact on overall portfolio returns (and even risk levels), regardless of how prudent investment committee members have been. These performance inhibitors, included below, are: unclear investment guidelines, diversification overload, time mismatch, poor communication, ineffective investment committees, too much useless information, and misleading and incomplete academic studies and articles.

PERFORMANCE INHIBITOR #1: UNCLEAR INVESTMENT GUIDELINES

The first of the performance inhibitors occurs when investment guidelines and stated goals and objectives are unclear or confusing. To an investment manager, these guidelines, if not articulated well, might be considered as constraints to their decision-making process. Any guideline that prevents the manager from creating alpha (the excess return over the benchmark) within the portfolio is considered a constraint in the mind of the manager. However, money managers generally expect their investment management agreement to outline some guidelines on the management of pension and investment assets. Money managers also realize that investment committee members are bound by their fiduciary responsibility to act in the best interests of the plan beneficiaries. It all forms part of the due-diligence process.

In fact, properly constructed guidelines give the money manager the necessary in-depth knowledge regarding the overall goals and objectives of the plan sponsor as they relate to performance expectations, risk tolerance, and time horizon. However, as pointed out in this section, if the investment guidelines are not properly constructed and explained, they could have a detrimental impact on performance results.

Pension fund and other institutional-type investors typically incorporate the investment guidelines within the investment management agreement under two main sections: portfolio criteria and performance standards.

Portfolio Criteria

There are three primary diversifying criteria for equity-oriented portfolios: sector allocation, security selection, and cash weighting.

1) Sector Allocation

Table 3.1 below shows the sector weightings within the four most common stock indexes used as benchmarks for measurement purposes:

TABLE 3.1: INDEXES

SECTOR	S&P 500 (%)	S&P/ TSX (%)	MSCI EAFE (%)	MSCI WORLD (%)
Communication Services	11	5	5	9
Consumer Discretionary	13	4	12	12
Consumer Staples	7	4	11	8
Energy	2	11	3	3
Financial Services	10	30	16	13
Healthcare	13	1	13	13
Industrials	8	13	15	10
Materials	3	14	8	5
Real Estate	2	3	3	3
Information Technology	28	10	9	22
Utilities	3	5	4	3
TOTAL	**100**	**100**	**100**	**100**

Sources: Standard & Poor's (S&P); Morgan Stanley Capital International (MSCI), as of December 31, 2020

From the 1960s through to the 1990s, it became common practice to place a maximum weighting of 25% on any one sector. This was a fairly safe limit, as no one sector represented more than 20% of the specific index at the time—giving managers some discretion to overweight any sector that they believed had above-average return potential. As shown in

Table 3.1 above, the world has changed. In the U.S. market, Information Technology now represents over one-fifth of the S&P 500 Index, followed closely by Healthcare at 13%, Consumer Discretionary at 13%, and Financial Services at 10% (these four sectors together represent just over 60% of the Index). In Canada, the market is skewed (more concentrated) slightly further with Financial Services accounting for 30% of the Index—with three sectors accounting for over a 55% weight. The MSCI EAFE and World indexes have a better balance (i.e., greater diversification, less concentration) across the 11 sectors—with only one sector in the World Index representing a weighting greater than 20%.

The larger sector weightings in some countries have created a risk profile of these indexes which might make them unacceptable as a measurement tool for gauging a manager's success or failure and, if left unconstrained for the money managers, might increase the risk exposure within the various portfolios under management. If we were to use the old rule of thumb of a maximum of 25% in any one sector, the manager would be at a significant disadvantage when the portfolio was measured against the S&P 500 and the S&P/TSX Composite indexes (the typical benchmarks for measuring managers' stock performance results for North American mandates). In this case, the manager would not be able to overweight some sectors. However, if higher maximum sector guidelines were included within the investment management agreement, risk levels might rise significantly above the tolerance level of the plan sponsor. This is a catch-22 situation.

The various country indexes have become an anchor from which sector weighting decisions are made. The big question from a fiduciary and overall prudence standpoint is: if we did not have any market indexes, but knew that there were 11 sectors within each country, what would investment committee members set as a reasonable guideline for sector exposure? I would guess that we would be back to a cap of 25% (at best) as a maximum for any one sector.

Surely, that the indexes have become more concentrated over time does not mean that the diversification critical for a portfolio should be lowered.

Changes in any index should not dictate an adjustment to investment prudence.

The decision here is for investment committee members to determine if there should be a specific cap on the weighting of any individual sector and, if so, what that weighting should be.

The investment committee has addressed risk at the asset mix level (including selecting various asset classes and asset class segments) and within the investment management structure (including managers with different investment styles and skills). As well, managers are not likely to deviate too far from the characteristics of the chosen benchmark—given either a low tracking error guideline or a low value-added target. Giving managers some greater latitude in allocating assets among the various sectors is not likely to change the risk profile at the total fund level.

2) Security Selection

The typical investment guideline for security selection is to place a maximum weighting on any individual holding within the portfolio. The intent is to provide some broad diversification among the securities held. The most common guideline maximum for an individual security within a portfolio is 10%. This is a fairly safe limit for any investment committee to impose, as it is also the maximum set by most regulatory authorities. Few, if any, managers would oppose this guideline, as it is also fairly standard within the managers' internal diversification guidelines that they have set for themselves.

The second most common individual security maximum is 7%. This is also not a major constraint, as it allows the managers to overweight, to some extent, most stocks within the various country indexes. By setting the weighting at 7% rather than 10%, the plan sponsor is sending a message to the money manager that individual portfolio diversification is important.

A further consideration is that if there is a need to ensure appropriate diversification within the portfolio, the investment committee might consider placing a maximum weight on the top 10 holdings within the portfolio. This limit could be capped at, for example, 40% of the market value of the portfolio. This cap might ensure that the portfolio does not become overly concentrated—if that is the desire.

3) Cash Weighting

Cash and short-term securities have lost their status since the 1980s as either an asset class or a defensive holding for market-timing purposes within segregated equity portfolios.

Currently, the most commonly accepted upper limit on the cash/short-term securities weighting within a segregated equity portfolio is 5%. With this limit, the investment committee is telegraphing to the managers that they are being "paid to play". If the manager has a bullish market outlook, it could adopt a more aggressive stance on security selection. If the manager is concerned about market levels, it could move the portfolio into a more defensive position through security selection—selecting stocks that may be less susceptible to a market correction, or shortening the term of the bond portfolio if interest rates are forecast to rise.

One exception to this 5% maximum cash weighting might be for investing in the small-cap segment of the marketplace (or some less liquid area of the market), which could be a constraint to a money manager. Small-cap mandates sometimes have a maximum average-cap size for the portfolio as a whole or for any individual holding that is allowed to be held within the portfolio. This guideline is to keep the integrity of the mandate intact. Holdings passing through the upper cap level might have to be sold, which could raise cash levels above 5%. Incidentally, small-cap managers, in any event, tend to hold a higher transitional weight in cash to take advantage of new or existing opportunities as they emerge. Perhaps a 10% maximum cash weighting could be considered for small-cap mandates. Another benefit of a slightly higher cash weighting for this area of the marketplace is that it lowers overall volatility.

The three portfolio criteria guidelines outlined above are all portfolio-specific. They are designed to reduce the risk exposure at the portfolio level. They may be included in the investment management agreement to ensure appropriate diversification within portfolios—and, more specifically, to provide comfort. However, these investment guidelines have become so commonplace that most money managers have incorporated them into their own internal diversification guidelines to demonstrate to plan sponsors, investors, and consultants that they have addressed the issue of risk management.

For fixed-income portfolios, specific guidelines might include a maximum weighting on corporate issues, a targeted duration level, a maximum exposure to high-yield securities, and an overall quality weighting.

Much focus has been placed on diversification guidelines for investment managers. Any constraints placed on the money manager should not inhibit the manager's ability to deliver alpha. That is basically what the manager has been hired to do. With a plethora of asset classes at the committee's disposal and various investment styles and approaches available, the need to broadly diversify individual portfolios has become significantly less important. Plan sponsors now place more emphasis on risk management at the total fund level, which allows money managers more latitude to seek out value-added returns.

When interviewing money manager candidates, investment committee members should ask them for their own internal investment guidelines, why they were chosen, whether they have changed over time and why, and whether they have negatively affected overall performance results.

PERFORMANCE STANDARDS

The second component of investment guidelines within the investment management agreement falls under the heading of performance standards. There are three issues that should be addressed here: selecting the appropriate benchmark, determining the value-added target, and stating the time horizon for performance measurement.

1) Designated Benchmark

As stated at the beginning of this chapter, the investment community is the most measured industry in the world—no other industry comes close. Plan sponsors can determine on a day-to-day basis whether managers are delivering on the stated goals and objectives. For measurement purposes, the process begins with selecting benchmarks that represent the targeted asset mix weightings at the total level, each asset class segment, and the individual portfolios managed by the managers.

According to CFA Institute:

A good composite benchmark has many of the following properties. It is:

- *specified in advance.* Although this may not always be the case, firms should select a composite benchmark prior to the evaluation period.

- *relevant.* The benchmark reflects the investment mandate, objectives, or strategy of the composite.

- *measurable.* The benchmark is quantifiable.

- *unambiguous.* The constituents of the investable universe can be clearly identified and priced.

- *representative of current investment opinions.* The firm has current knowledge of the investable universe.

- *accountable.* The firm selects the benchmark and is accountable for any deviations from the benchmark.

- *investable.* The benchmark offers a passive alternative that is a realizable and alternative opportunity genuinely open to the investor.

- *complete.* The benchmark provides a broad representation of the sector of the market to which it pertains.

Finally, "choosing a bad or inappropriate benchmark can undermine the effectiveness of an investment strategy and lead to dissatisfaction between client and manager."

For the money manager, the chosen benchmark acts as a telltale—basically, outlining the main universe for security selection. This benchmark should be agreed to by the investment committee, the money manager, and, perhaps, the consultant.

2) Valued-Added Target

Of the three factors addressed under Performance Standards within the investment management agreement, an appropriate value-added target is the most difficult to determine—and often involves the least amount of effective communication between the investment committee, the consultant, and the money manager. The investment committee members (and, perhaps, even the consultant) commonly believe that if the value-added target is not set high enough, the manager won't try as hard to deliver performance results. Meanwhile, the manager prefers a low value-added target to increase the odds of achieving the plan sponsor's desired goals and objectives.

It is important to spend the time to get the value-added target right as it typically highlights the risk tolerance and appetite of the plan sponsor for the money manager. If the value-added target is set at, say, 50 basis points above the S&P 500 Index over a specified time period, the target might signal to the manager that the client is somewhat risk averse and is looking for a more core/index-like portfolio. If the value-added target is set at 150 basis points over this Index, the target might indicate to the manager that the plan sponsor is more aggressive, willing to take on greater risk and volatility, and looking for a more concentrated (bigger bets) portfolio. Basically, the larger the value-added target, the greater the risk acceptance—at least, that is the way it will be interpreted. The problem arises when the investment committee sets a value-added target too high and, as a result, changes the money manager's portfolio focus—perhaps taking on more risk than intended.

Setting a value-added target can sometimes contradict the beliefs of the plan sponsor based on initial meetings with the manager. Assume that the manager was told that the investment committee members had a very conservative bent (for the right reasons) and did not want a lot of volatility in the portfolio around the benchmark (resulting in a relatively low tracking error to the benchmark), yet the plan sponsor sets the value-added target at 200 basis points above the S&P 500 Index. This value-added target would telegraph a relatively high risk appetite. The more constraining the guidelines, the lower the value-added target should be. However, in reality, the guidelines and targets are very seldom effectively linked.

In my role as an investment planning consultant, our firm had just been hired by a pension client that had given its money manager full discretion to be invested 100% in either the U.S. equity market or the Canadian equity market—based on the manager's expectations about which market provided the greater opportunity. Furthermore, based on the previous consultant's recommendation, the client had given the manager a value-added target of 400 basis points (no, that is not a typo) over the S&P 500 Index, or the S&P/TSX Composite Index—based on whichever market the money manager was in at the time (there was no blended benchmark). The manager was "all-in" in one market or the other. Each quarter, the manager would present his portfolio strategy to the investment committee. Each quarter, the manager talked about all the great opportunities within the U.S. marketplace. Yet, each quarter, the manager would show the portfolio being 100% invested in Canadian securities. In my second meeting with the money manager and client, I asked why he seemed to like the U.S. market, but was exclusively invested in Canada. The manager responded that he did not believe he could come close to achieving the valued-added target objective of 400 basis points above either index; however, he felt that there was a better chance of coming closer in Canada. This one decision—setting an unachievable high value-added target—forced the manager to deviate from his normal portfolio strategy and incurred an opportunity cost within the client's pension plan valued at well over $10 million over a three-year period.

The value-added target should be set in conjunction with the plan sponsor, the money manager, and the consultant. If set too high, it could trigger firing the money manager when performance is below the target, which, given the market conditions at the time, might not be warranted. It is important to get the value-added target right. This target must be mandate-specific.

3) Time Horizon

As difficult as it might be to determine a fair and reasonable value-added target, setting the time horizon is likely the easiest task. The consensus timeframe for performance measurement seems to be over four-year moving-average time periods.

Setting a four-year time horizon is important only at the start of the client-manager relationship. After four years have passed, performance should be measured on a since-inception basis—capturing all market cycles. The investment committee will want to determine, over time, how its money manager performs in up and down markets. If the manager performs well in bear markets, protecting capital value, the investment committee should not be surprised by relatively good results in the next down cycle. Furthermore, in a speculative market, a manager may be expected to underperform given its style, approach, and decision-making process. Time confirms whether the manager selection process works (or not). It is rare for a money manager to deliver above-average performance in both significant up- and down-market cycles.

Selecting an appropriate time horizon should also be mandate-specific. For core/market-oriented portfolios, a timeframe of four years may be appropriate. However, for investment mandates that are non-core or within specific market niches (e.g., small cap, real estate, venture capital, infrastructure, and high yield), the measurement time horizon should be longer to give the more non-traditional asset classes time to work out. The more concentrated or non-core the investment mandate, the longer the time horizon should be. This, of course, does not mean that money managers should not be tracked, monitored, and evaluated over shorter time periods.

As stated earlier, the setting of overall investment guidelines should be undertaken jointly by all three parties: the plan sponsor, the money manager, and the consultant. The guidelines should be fair, reasonable, achievable, and unconstrained. The consultant's role is to educate and advise investment committee members and the money manager so that both are on the same page—reducing the chances of any surprises down the road. The consultant must be an effective and unbiased intermediary in this process—understanding the goals of the plan sponsor and the ability and skills of the money manager.

One last point is worth noting: the investment committee should inform their managers that if any investment management agreement guideline proves to be too restrictive within a specific market cycle, given the manager's decision-making process and its market outlook, it should feel free to bring this to the attention of the committee members. The committee can then make the call as to whether the guideline should be temporarily adjusted. The investment committee members have a better handle on the overall risk tolerance of the investment fund, as their focus is on risk management at the total fund level as well as within each asset class segment.

In summary, the benchmark must be appropriate for the specific mandate of the plan sponsor, the value-added target will represent the risk tolerance, and the timeframe will indicate the tolerance for short-term underperformance. The timeframe is the least important, as monitoring and evaluation is on ongoing process.

PERFORMANCE INHIBITOR #2: INEFFECTIVE DIVERSIFICATION

Fulfilling the duties of a fiduciary requires acting in a prudent manner. The various regulatory authorities consider prudence in administering and managing pension and investment funds as having appropriate diversification. However, diversification by itself is not a guarantee of prudence. Prudence can also be defined as the process by which the investment committee exercises its responsibilities throughout the investment program.

Table 3.2 below shows the various levels of diversification, indicating which party is responsible for setting the diversification guidelines at each level, as well as my "best guess" as to the impact that these levels may have on total fund performance:

TABLE 3.2: LEVELS OF DIVERSIFICATION

SIX DEGREES OF DIVERSIFICATION	APPROXIMATE PERCENTAGE IMPACT	PRIMARY RESPONSIBILITY
Asset Mix Allocation	> 90%	Sponsor/Consultant
Geographic Regions	2–3%	Sponsor/Consultant
Manager/Style/Approach	< 1%	Sponsor/Consultant
Time	< 1%	Sponsor/Consultant
Sector Weighting	< 1%	Money Manager
Security Selection	< 1%	Money Manager

As shown in Table 3.2 above, the decisions at the plan sponsor level dominate and are likely to account for over 95% of the impact of these diversification levels on the overall fund performance—with the money management level having a fairly minor role to play. Thus, the decisions of the plan sponsor have a major impact on overall fund performance. As indicated in Chapter Two, well over 90% of the overall fund return might be attributed to the asset mix decision while virtually all of the risk can be attributed to asset mix policy.

First Degree: Asset Mix Allocation

The plan sponsor, as the administrator, has to deliver a sufficient rate of return to provide for the longer-term payout of the obligations (promises) outlined in the pension plan and other legal documents. Meanwhile, the fiduciary responsibility of the plan sponsor is to act in a prudent manner—which typically focuses on providing appropriate diversification at the total fund level to reduce overall risk. Reducing overall risk is easier, and more predictable, than seeking the desired returns. Getting the balance right is the ongoing responsibility of the plan sponsor.

The investment policy decision includes determining which asset classes to include within the investment management structure; the policy, target, or neutral asset mix weightings for each asset class; the tolerance ranges on either side of the policy mix; and the amount of discretion given to each manager within the investment program.

In summary, the first level of diversification, the asset mix, is the responsibility of the plan sponsor. As prudence is typically defined by appropriate diversification, there is a tendency to include as many asset classes and asset class segments as possible—as the vast majority of risk management (reducing overall volatility) is determined at the asset mix level. The good news is that asset classes are fairly easy to define.

Bottom line: The most important decision affecting overall diversification is getting the appropriate weighting between ownership-type assets and fixed-income securities. However, each asset class has its own return patterns and volatility levels. If correlations are high between one asset class and another, the diversification benefit might be muted. Too many asset classes just might be too many.

Second Degree: Geographic Regions

Investing has become a lot more complicated. It was far easier when the world was flat. Now, investing has gone global. We are investing in countries with different languages, different accounting systems (if any exist at all), different economic, political, and social environments, different economic growth patterns, different industries and companies, different currencies, etc. However, this is one area of diversification in which the reward for exposure outside a specific domestic market may be as attractive as the benefits of risk reduction.

Geographic allocation adds a new dimension to the decision-making process in constructing the equity segment within the investment management structure, as shown in the following Figure 3.1:

FIGURE 3.1: INVESTMENT FOCUS

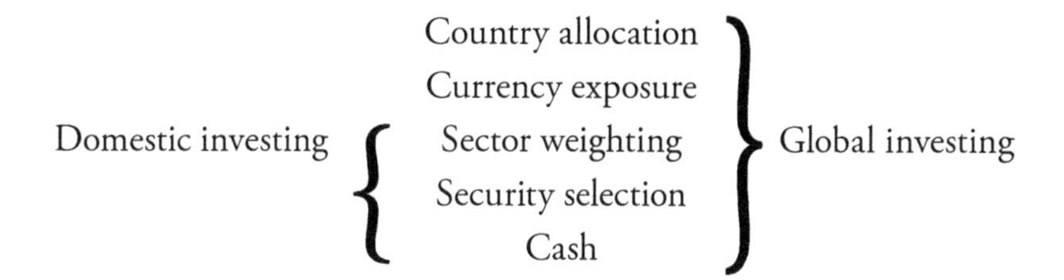

Investment managers, operating within their own domestic market, focus on what sectors, industries, and companies they believe will provide above-average performance, and then attempt to identify and select the best stocks within each sector. The cash weighting is generally for market-timing purposes (protecting portfolio values in a down market), a residual of the decision-making process (a build-up when securities are sold and reduced when securities are bought), or a contingency allocation if the portfolio is in a redemption phase—with monies being withdrawn from the fund on a regular scheduled basis. However, remember that cash or cash equivalents held within an equity portfolio are considered a separate asset class and, in rising markets (which is most of the time), are always a drag on returns.

For the global manager, two more layers come into play: country allocation and currency exposure. The currency exposure can be eliminated or reduced by a hedging process. However, overall diversification may benefit from exposing the fund to various currencies around the world.

There are many benefits of geographic distribution:

1. the correlation of returns from non-North American markets is lower, which works best for weaker economic ties (e.g., U.S.–Canada correlation is higher than that of other major markets around the world, owing to their closely linked economies);

2. the economies of some non-North American countries are growing faster than domestic markets—this is especially true within emerging markets;

3. some large industries and companies are not represented significantly in the North American economies—and, therefore, have a positive impact on diversification at the security level; and,

4. the addition of various currencies can provide another level of diversification with the potential to lower the overall volatility of the fund.

In summary, diversification by geographic region is certain to reduce the risk level of a fund. It also provides an opportunity to enhance total fund returns in the process—a win/win situation for the plan sponsor.

Third Degree: Investment Manager, Investment Style, and Investment Approach

Selecting active money managers to manage the various asset classes is one of the most important decisions an investment committee can make—it is also one of the most difficult activities to undertake.

Beginning in the mid-1980s, plan sponsors began to diversify asset class segments by the various investment styles of the money managers to offer further diversification within an asset class. In theory, investment style diversification assumes that a) one manager's screening process (either quantitative or qualitative), investment approach, decision-making process, and focus can be significantly different from another's, and b) that combining two or more money managers with different investment styles typically results in lower volatility at the total fund level and within the specific asset class. If done correctly, it might even deliver higher returns—the hoped-for outcome.

As discussed in Chapter Two, there are three primary investment styles (i.e., growth, value, and market oriented) used in the creation of stock portfolios. However, there are two caveats related to style analysis: first, not all markets can be neatly divided into these styles (e.g., Canada cannot, owing to its heavy concentration in financials and resources). The less liquid and more concentrated a market, the less likely style offsets will work. Second, a growth style and a value style are not at opposite ends of the style spectrum; they are just two different focuses in the construction of portfolios. One focuses primarily on company fundamentals (growth style) while the other focuses primarily on market statistics (value style).

For fixed-income mandates, diversification refers to bond market segments and is based more on strategy than style. Bond managers generally seek out market anomalies within *quality* and *time*. There are two basic sectors within the fixed-income market: 1) government and quasi-government bond issues, and 2) corporate bond issues and other non-government bond issues. Bond managers may specialize in one or the other of these sectors. The quality level of individual bond issuers and issues is rated by several rating service agencies that specialize in tracking influencing factors affecting the quality level of a specific issuer or issue. The ratings typically fall into two major categories: investment-grade bond ratings (e.g., AAA, AA, A, BBB—with some pluses and minuses thrown in for good luck), and below-investment-grade bond ratings (i.e., lower than BBB). Issues that fall into the below-investment-grade status are generally referred to as "high-yield securities" or the unflattering term "junk bonds." Quality levels are distinguished by the yield spreads from one level to another, or from one issuer or issue to another. For government-like issues, the spreads can be quite narrow, while for investment-grade corporates, the spreads tend to widen out a bit, and become even wider still for issues that fall into the below-investment-grade area.

There are three main bond strategies: sector rotation, security selection, and interest-rate anticipation.

Some bond managers fall into a *sector-rotation* category—where the main strategy is to switch from one sector of the bond market to another based on the relative yield spreads between the various sectors and on the manager's outlook for how these spreads might change over time. If the manager expects the economy to weaken, the *sector rotator* might purchase government issues with the expectation that yields will widen against corporate issues. If the manager expects the economy to improve, the trade might be reversed with the spreads favoring corporates.

The second main strategy to enhance bond portfolio returns is individual *security selection*. With this strategy, bond managers focus on credit analysis to determine the quality levels between individual securities. When spreads between lower-quality issues narrow against higher-quality issues, the bond manager may choose to increase the quality of the portfolio, as the risk of holding the lower-quality issues does not compensate the manager given the expected return. When spreads widen, the bond manager may lower the quality within the portfolio. As a result, the investor is hoping to be well compensated for taking this additional risk.

The third main bond strategy is to forecast interest-rate trends. If interest rates were expected to decline within the selected time horizon, the bond manager might elect to lengthen the duration or average term of the bond portfolio—as these issues benefit most when interest rates fall. If interest rates were expected to increase, the manager might elect to shorten the duration of the portfolio to protect capital value. Managers attempting to time the market are referred to as *interest-rate anticipators*. Managers who attempt to take advantage of shifts in the yield curve also fall within this category. The yield curve is always shifting and can provide bond managers with an opportunity to add value to their portfolios.

The approach to *high-yield investing* is altogether different. The focus here is on the fundamentals of the corporations and other entities issuing these securities. High-yield securities are more affected by economic events and the profitability of the corporation or entity issuing the debt. The in-depth research analysis is more like that of equity managers than fixed-income managers. The volatility of this segment of the marketplace is also closer to that of stocks. In addition, these issues have a default premium built into the overall yield along with an illiquidity premium. Over the past few decades, the high-yield market has performed well—compensating investors for the higher risk.

In summary, the benefits of diversification at the level of the investment manager are not as clear-cut as they are at the first two levels (asset class allocation and geographic diversification); however, without overdoing the style-offset effort, diversification at this level is a value-added proposition. Each money manager organization has its own team "signature" in portfolio creation. When selecting more than one money manager for an asset class (e.g., global equities), the greater the overlap of securities held within each portfolio the less the diversification benefit.

Fourth Degree: Time

Time, the fourth degree of diversification, is not as easy to quantify as the first three levels; however, time is no less important than the other areas of diversification within an investment portfolio. Time needs to be considered at two levels: the plan sponsor (policy) and the money manager (strategy).

The plan sponsor, with the necessary input from the consulting actuary, must determine whether the pension or investment fund itself has a short-, medium-, or longer-term time horizon. Typically, factors such as the average age of the participants, the type of plan, the ratio of current members to retirees, and the type of organization (e.g., government vs. corporate) significantly impact the selection and weighting of the various asset classes. The main focus of the plan sponsor is on the asset mix and the allocation to ownership-type assets versus a fixed-income exposure. Typically, the longer the time horizon, the higher the risk tolerance, which presents an opportunity for a higher equity component.

Most defined-benefit pension plans and other types of investment funds in North America have a longer-term time horizon. As a result, for most pension and investment funds, the equity exposure tends to be at or above 60% of the overall fund—as determined by investment policy. The odds are in favor of a longer time horizon for funds, as the shorter-term volatile of returns move closer to the longer-term trend line over time. In other words, the longer the time horizon, the less likely there will be a negative accumulative return on the equity segment.

The fixed-income manager is also a partner in setting the appropriate duration of the plan sponsor's fund. There is no use determining that the pension fund has a longer-term time horizon at the total fund level if the fixed-income manager holds only short- to mid-term bonds. The fixed-income manager must know the expectations of the plan sponsor and, perhaps matching more closely the duration of the fixed-income portfolio to the duration of the pension assets.

In summary, time plays an important role in determining asset class selection and the weightings assigned to each asset class. Typically, the longer the time horizon, the higher the percentage that can be allocated to ownership-type investments.

Fifth Degree: Sector Weighting

As stated earlier in this chapter, fund diversification is the responsibility of three parties: the plan sponsor, the consultant, and the money manager. All three parties should be involved in the first four degrees, as each has a different perspective on the meaning of diversification. It is important for each party to understand the role it plays in reducing the fund's overall risk, while aiming to achieve the return expectations. The fifth degree, sector weighting, is implemented by the investment manager.

The money manager, within either a growth or a value investment style, typically chooses to be in most of the 11 sectors—if not all of them. Even if a manager were told to focus on seeking returns, the manager would know that deviating too far from the benchmark might be a career-ending exercise. There are two approaches for money managers to determine sector weights. The first is driven by the manager's top–down approach, on a primarily qualitative and quantitative basis. Here, the manager is focused either on the various economic variables that impact the growth or value factors for each sector, or on various screening techniques to assess the relative attractiveness of each sector. Given the expectations, the money manager weights these sectors accordingly.

The second approach to achieve the sector weighting is the residual of a bottom–up, security selection process. The primary focus here is on security selection. Here, whatever style, approach, or decision-making process is used by the investment manager in constructing a portfolio, the sector weighting is a secondary consideration. However, even when the focus is exclusively on bottom–up security selection, there is typically some maximum guideline for the overall weighting of a sector (e.g., a maximum weighting in any one sector of 25%, or a maximum 110% on any sector with a weighting greater than 20% in the specific index/benchmark—giving the money manager some flexibility).

In summary, the various indexes used as benchmarks have become more concentrated by sector since the early 2000s. Concentration can lead to greater volatility. Greater volatility within the benchmark could result in greater risk exposure at the total fund level.

Sixth Degree: Security Selection

Today, the concept of diversification permeates the decision-making process, not only at the plan sponsor level, but also at the money manager level. The emphasis on prudence, previously within the realm of the plan sponsor, has now been incorporated at the money management level as well—not that money managers were not prudent in the past, just that the standards have changed. The primary consideration today, when new monies arrive at the manager's desk, is how to diversify the portfolio immediately in a prudent manner. Return enhancement is not as great a focus by the money manager as it once was. It could also be that return enhancement is not as easy to come by as it used to be.

As stated earlier in this chapter, unless mandated, concentrated portfolios are a rarity. This has occurred for four reasons:

1. pension and other investment assets managed by money management firms have grown significantly and the resulting liquidity constraints have made it quite difficult to construct concentrated portfolios;

2. although the primary emphasis has moved from peer-group comparisons to market-oriented benchmark measurement, risk/reward charts (the scatter diagram) still receive attention, and investment committee members still want to see the returns of their portfolios placed neatly within the northwest quadrant—it is human nature to be curious, to see how well we performed against our neighbor, possibly hoping for bragging rights;

3. money managers do not believe they will be rewarded for taking more aggressive bets owing to the increasing turnover rate of money managers by plan sponsors, and the emphasis on a shorter time horizon for achieving superior returns; and,

4. on the positive side, there are a lot more stocks to select from now that the universe has moved from a domestic focus to global coverage.

Diversification at the money manager level has taken on a new dimension. In general, funds have become much more broadly diversified. Does this mean that a manager's investment style has changed? Not necessarily. The following tests can be applied to observe whether a portfolio's concentration bets have changed over time:

1. check whether the number of securities held within a portfolio has increased over the past decade;

2. assess whether the weighting of the top 10 securities held has diminished over the past decade; and,

3. determine whether the average capitalization of the portfolio has increased against a market benchmark over the same period of time.

These changes to a more broadly diversified portfolio may result in a lower value-added return in the future than what was delivered in the past.

In summary, diversification has become the predominant way of life within the plan sponsor community as well as at the money management level. The plan sponsor cannot be faulted for taking the diversification route over the return-enhancement route, as prudence is now defined by the consensus view of diversification. The plan sponsor can play it safe. In fact, the investment committee does not make the decision to de-emphasize the return side of the equation; rather, this result is more of a residual from the primary focus on diversification.

We know that the benefits of diversification—the "known knowns." However, there may be ways of enhancing returns through more aggressive strategies at the money management level that do not significantly impact the total fund's overall risk profile. Plan sponsors should be responsible for determining the appropriate risk tolerance and appetite, then focus primarily on risk management at the total fund level. Investment managers should be encouraged, where and when appropriate, to move back to their role of being return seekers to enhance overall results at the total portfolio level.

If, as studies have shown, well over 90% of the return and volatility of a portfolio is determined by the plan sponsor through its decisions on asset mix, geographic regions, manager selection, and term management, then money managers, on their worst days, would not have a major impact on increasing the risk profile of the total fund. However, money managers seeking returns can have a significant positive impact on returns. They simply need to be given the appropriate guidelines, performance standards, and time. My formula for investment success is:

Investment success = homework + commitment + patience

One caveat: at some point, too much diversification may negatively impact overall returns more than it reduces overall risks. As a precaution, the investment committee shouldn't over-diversify the total fund right into the fourth quartile on a peer-group comparison.

PERFORMANCE INHIBITOR #3: THE TIME WARP

In the investment world, time has a major influence on investment decisions. Almost all investment actions are analyzed, measured, and judged within a specified timeframe. Although a pension fund typically has a longer-term time horizon, actuaries undertake pension plan valuations every three years at a minimum. Regarding corporate pension funds, accountants calculate liabilities (a balance sheet item) and pension costs (an earnings statement item) yearly, while pension administrators review fund performance from their investment managers quarterly. These are the major players that influence the activities within the investment program.

Our culture has devolved to the point where we have a short-term focus on almost everything we do. Studies have shown that the average security holding period for U.S. equity mutual funds has shortened from around four to five years in the 1960s to closer to one year today. I believe this "short-termism" has a detrimental impact on the overall performance of investment portfolios—be they for pension funds, operating and endowment funds, foundations, or individuals. I also believe that short-termism results in costs rising, risks increasing, and returns suffering—the worst of all worlds.

Figure 3.2 below outlines the estimated timelines that I believe apply to various parties that influence investment decisions—based on my experience as a money manager, plan sponsor, and investment planning consultant:

FIGURE 3.2: TIME MISMATCH OF DIFFERENT PARTIES

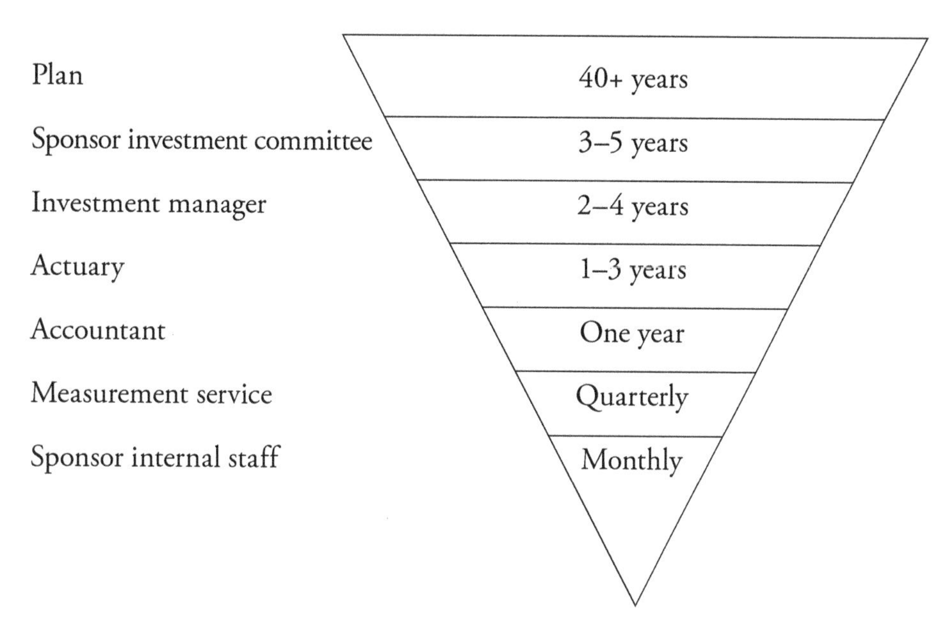

The diagram shows that the major players do not operate in the same time zone—and there is very little overlap from one time focus to another.

The Pension Plan

The pension plan is our starting point. With the assistance of the actuary, corporations, government-sponsored organizations, and other such investment-oriented entities have become plan sponsors. For a defined-benefit plan, the plan sponsor makes certain promises, whereby, at the end of plan members' working careers, funds will be available to provide a pension income to the members and their beneficiaries for their lifetimes. The primary advantage of a defined-benefit plan for a pensioner is a known quantity of funds that continue for life, however long.

There are two primary reasons for a time period of 40-plus years for corporate pension plans (the time period for government-sponsored plans is typically longer). First, the plan beneficiaries work for about 40 years (usually retiring in their early 60s—although this is changing as baby boomers are retiring a little later in life). Second, the plan sponsor usually operates in an industry with a long-term future (which is now not as common as it used to be). When pension plans were first set up, workers were mainly employed by one company for their entire working careers (getting the gold watch and pension at the end), and companies (mostly manufacturing firms) had staying power. However, the North American economy has changed significantly since the 1960s: it has moved from a manufacturing base (with workers earning higher annual wages) to a service-based economy (with lower wages). Basically, the economy has moved from building big bridges, to building big autos, to building big buildings, and now, to building Big Macs.

The Sponsor Investment Committee

Investment committee members have the fiduciary responsibility to link all pension fund activities to the goals and objectives of the pension plan as a whole. Given human nature and the challenges of predicting the future, it is difficult for investment committee members to look out more than three to five years down the road—especially in this day and age when geo-political events, economic factors, and the investment environment are changing so rapidly. However, this time plane may be a significant mismatch to that of the fund itself.

The Investment Manager

As mentioned earlier in this chapter, the time horizon for measuring investment managers should be well defined and set out in the investment management agreement. The most common stated time horizon for manager assessments and evaluations has typically been rolling four-year periods. Benchmarks and peer-group samples have come and gone, and value-added targets and placements have changed over the years, but this four-year time horizon has remained fairly constant. However, we continue to move away from the longevity of the pension plan.

Even though the time horizon is generally stated as four years, money managers know that, in reality, the time period for them being fired can be significantly shorter. The consequences of being judged by plan administrators over shorter-term time horizons has resulted in money managers changing their own investment time horizon from the historical level of three to five years some decades ago to more like two to three years today—once again, moving the industry further away from the long-term nature of the pension fund. For example, there has never been as clear a focus by investors on short-term corporate earnings results as there is today. Earnings results falling short or exceeding expectations by even a cent or two could move a stock up or down by 5% or more.

The Actuary

The pension plan does not start without the actuary. In most jurisdictions, plan valuations must be completed at least every three years. Some plan sponsors may do so more often, depending on their funded status, contribution requirements, benefits offered, and the stage of the capital market cycle. The 2000s proved to be an extremely difficult decade for the pension fund industry, starting with the second-worst recession since the Great Depression and finishing with the worst recession. Liabilities were increasingly forced to a mark-to-market basis, at low discount rates, and ballooned as a result. Pension surpluses in the 1990s quickly became pension deficits in the 2000s. The situation has improved with the strong equity markets of the 2010s.

Although investment policy should be founded on a carefully structured asset/liability risk perspective (not asset-only), each successive actuarial evaluation should not, in the majority of cases, result in major changes to investment policy or strategy. Again, these are short-term snapshots within a long-term evolution.

The Accountant

The accountant for many years was off on the sidelines, but, finally, the accounting industry has been convinced (not least by the investment professions) that pension liabilities should be put on corporate balance sheets, and the variance between the liabilities promised and the actual funded position should be included in the earnings statements. The result is that the operating business of the corporate plan sponsor may now be affected, on an annual basis, by an asset with a very long-term time horizon. Corporations, typically, attempt to smooth out the volatility of their bottom line. If the variance from the pension fund increases bottom-line volatility, corporations are highly motivated to abandon their defined-benefit plans in favor of defined-contribution plans, or to de-risk the pension fund—both outcomes are a significant detriment to plan beneficiaries.

Accounting requirements have now introduced a significantly shorter timeframe of one year for corporate plan sponsors to review pension fund activity. The result is likely to be a more conservative approach in investing corporate pension fund monies.

The Measurement Service

Performance measurement services provide plan sponsors with performance information every quarter. Now, performance measurement is not a bad thing—in spite of what money managers say. People visit their doctors regularly to make sure that everything is still in the right place and functioning as it should. Transparency and explanations are owed to plan sponsors and beneficiaries alike. However, way too much attention is paid to the quarterly numbers, and decisions based on short-term results are typically detrimental to the longer-term performance of a pension fund—as short-term performance results are basically random.

The Plan Sponsor/Internal Staff

In recent years, more plan sponsors are now seeking and tracking total fund and money manager returns every month. This trend may be the result of hedge fund managers being able to track their performance on a month-by-month basis—the assumption being that if hedge fund managers can do it, why can't traditional money managers? A monthly assessment may work for some hedge fund managers, but it does not generally work for traditional money managers who, ideally, are investing for the long term rather than speculating over the short term. Investment managers take cues from investment committee members—sometimes without the members even realizing that they have influenced the manager's mindset.

In summary, as highlighted in Figure 3.2 above, no party operates within the same time zone—there is a significant misalignment. To be prudent going forward, and to provide the best opportunity for enhancing returns and managing risk, the investment committee members must address this "time warp." Focusing on the shorter term is costing the pension and investment industry way too much money, time, and effort. Investment committee members should make every effort to develop policy for the long term and to vary strategy only when plan characteristics change or markets move to extremes. Money managers should be given mandates with explicit long-term objectives and with aligned compensation arrangements. Then, managers should be given more time to perform within reasonable pre-set boundaries—as long as there has been no ownership changes, key personnel departures, or style change of the money manager. Short-term performance should be among the last reasons for terminating a money manager relationship—if the manager is conducting itself and its processes in the expected manner.

If a money management organization believes that its relationship with the plan sponsor (and the consultant) is a partnership, then the manager may feel more confident to invest with a longer-term vision of opportunities within the market. This belief has three beneficial outcomes:

1. the money manager is less likely to turn the portfolio over as often, resulting in more monies retained within the portfolio;
2. the firing of money managers before their time may be reduced—yielding savings of up to 1% (or even more) in the transition costs of the portfolio segment the manager was responsible for; and,
3. investment capital is directed to companies with the best long-term fundamental prospects (not the best short-term stock price expectations).

PERFORMANCE INHIBITOR #4: DEFECTIVE COMMUNICATION

In the new millennium, relationship management has become a popular term when referring to the relationship liaison between the plan sponsor and the money manager. Relationship management represents the desire to move to a higher plane. It is a holistic approach to client servicing that seeks a closer, more productive, and effective partnership between the investment committee and money manager. However, in the rush to get it right, we cannot forget that the foundation of good relationship management is effective communication.

Communication Factors

Communication is an easy word to define and it is commonly accepted that it is important in everyday life. Webster's Dictionary defines communication as "a process by which information is exchanged between individuals through a common system of symbols, signs, and behaviors." Effective communication is an attitude—of mutual trust and respect, understanding, and confidence between the parties. This is especially true in the management and administration of investment assets. If this confidence level is missing, no matter how good the performance of the money manager might be, it may not satisfy the plan sponsor. Meanwhile, in an environment in which communication is constructive, poor performance may be tolerated in the short term, if the investment committee members have a clear understanding of the manager's style and why the performance targets have not been met in the current investment environment.

Poor communication is fairly easy to measure. Poor communication causes rifts between spouses, parents and children, corporate management and staff, governments and voters, governments and governments, etc. Good communication, meanwhile, is somewhat difficult to measure, and, therefore, does not get the credit it might deserve. Of course, even great communication could always be better. In the investment management industry, one problem with poor communication is that it is usually recognized by the money manager only when it is too late.

Poor communication could even affect a fund's investment outcome. A breakdown in communication between the investment committee members, the investment manager, and the consultant could result in the dilution of overall investment returns and/or an unacceptable risk level.

Effective communication breaks down between the plan sponsor and investment managers for the following reasons:

- *Time*: Today, time is scarce. In our "microwave society", we are on call 24/7. We rush from one place to another. There is very little downtime. The primary plan sponsor contact has more and more non-investment-related activities pushed their way. Due to scheduling conflicts, it becomes increasingly difficult to have frequent in-depth meetings with the various service providers, especially the money managers—there are fewer meetings and less time for each meeting. The problem is that neither party gets to know the other as well as it should. A lack of understanding can create conflict. The relationship between the plan sponsor and the manager must be formed as a partnership.

- *Focus*: Corporate plan sponsors and some institutional-type investors have been trained in long-term corporate planning. Pension liabilities are obligations that are usually due many years in the future. Meanwhile, the investment manager has been trained to respond to short-term stimuli—quickly responding to an ever-changing investment climate caused by fluctuating trends in the economic, political, and social landscapes that affect market valuations. The focus of the plan sponsor is on longer-term *secular* trends, while that of the investment manager is on shorter-term *cyclical* trends.

  Investment policy (directed by the plan sponsor) is typically designed for the longer term (10-plus years), while investment strategy (implemented by the investment manager) is typically designed for the shorter term (two to three years). Somewhere within this range, common ground has to be found.

- *Message:* Every investment committee meeting contains "messages"—some explicit and some implicit; some intentional and some unintentional. Investment committee members may be sending mixed signals to an investment manager without realizing it.

  In my role within an investment management firm, one of our clients decided to raise its equity exposure from 50% to 60% on the recommendation of its investment planning consultant. Our mandate at the time was a balanced/multi-class fund. As the meeting was wrapping up, the chairperson asked me to remain behind for further discussion (never a good sign—like being called into the principal's office at school). The chairperson was uncomfortable with raising the equity weight to 60% given his views of the stock market. However, the other committee members expected us to come back to the next meeting with an increased weighting in equities. This created a disconnect between the chairperson and the other committee members. This is a no-win situation for the money manager. Furthermore, what is not said could be as important as what is said. Managers attempt to read the body language of the members of investment committees to determine their comfort level; however, they don't always get it right.

- *Personalities:* Not everyone is going to get along. Personality conflicts do arise and could damage an otherwise ideal investment relationship between the plan sponsor and the investment manager. If the plan sponsor finds it difficult to deal with one or two individuals within the money management firm, substitutes should be found. For the money manager, there are generally two levels of contact. The first is the point-person of the plan sponsor, who administers and monitors day-to-day activities. The second level is the investment committee members. The needs and wants of these two levels are different. The point-person (often referred to as the "gatekeeper") is likely to have a closer relationship with the money managers and have a better understanding of their decision-making process. The investment committee members tend to only see money managers in performance review sessions, resulting in significantly less frequent contact.

Unfortunately, personality conflicts are not easy to remedy. They can escalate quickly and are almost impossible to fix. Money management organizations are quite willing to change the contact if it would mean retaining the account. The plan sponsor just has to be open and honest.

- *Expectations:* If a manager is underperforming, it is quite natural for investment committee members to be frustrated—this outcome is the result of human nature and is not unexpected. After all, the reputations of investment committee members are also on the line, as the committee was responsible for hiring the manager in the first place.

Some managers can be out of sync with the market and their peer group for an extended period of time. It does not necessarily mean that the money manager woke up one morning not knowing what it is doing. Things happen. During these periods of disappointing results, good communication skills and reasonable expectations are critical. Investment managers must be forthcoming about the reasons for performance weakness, while plan sponsors should know that a stern tongue-lashing would make little difference. Money management organizations internally rate each of their clients on a scale of "safe" to "at risk." They know when they are on the ropes.

The goal of the investment committee members should be to have a deeper understanding of the portfolio so that the proper "retain or fire" decision can be made.

I created the following formula for determining happiness at the plan sponsor level:

Investor happiness = Performance, expectations - Reality

If reality exceeds expectations, the manager is safe and the plan sponsor is happy.

The investment committee members must ensure that there is effective communication with all the service providers to the pension or investment fund. It is the committee's responsibility to develop proper processes and procedures throughout the investment program.

In summary, a lack of effective communication with the money managers can result in a detrimental impact on performance or a lack of trust and confidence in the manager, which might trigger the firing of the manager for the wrong reasons.

PERFORMANCE INHIBITOR #5: DYSFUNCTIONAL INVESTMENT COMMITTEES

There are four main influences at the investment committee level that can have a detrimental impact on overall portfolio performance:

- *Membership*: For medium- to smaller-sized pension and investment funds, investment committee members are typically drawn from the plan participants. The rationale is that plan participants have a vested interest in the outcome of decisions made by the committee and, therefore, are expected to act in the best interests of all involved—a quite reasonable assumption. However, the vast majority (if not all) of the members of most investment committees have little to no experience related to the investment field. Investment committees should have at least one member who is a seasoned investment professional—someone who, preferably, has the CFA designation, or a minimum of 20 years of experience in the investment industry. The most effective committees have members who understand the investment field, grasp their role as committee members, understand the expertise required to effectively hire service providers to assist in developing and implementing the investment program, and have the time to fulfill their fiduciary responsibilities. Without experienced committee members, an effective chairperson, and appropriate monitoring and evaluation processes and procedures, mistakes are likely to be made—and they are likely to be significant. There must be accountability at the investment committee level. The investment field has become a lot more complicated over the past two to three decades, putting a lot more pressure on committee members to understand how these changes may affect their ongoing role as committee members. Membership on an investment committee is no longer a part-time position, and no longer without scrutiny.

- *Time Horizon*: If the average age of the committee members is around 60 years, the members' timeframe for foreseeing the future might be significantly shorter than what the plan allows—a longer-term time horizon favoring the patient investor. Over the years, and in my role as an investment planning consultant, I have consulted to many multi-employer plans—with an equal number of investment committee members from the management side and the union side. In most cases, union members are elected by their constituents for a specific term. Getting re-elected is foremost in many of their minds, as being on an investment committee has certain perks (e.g., attending seminars and visiting money manager offices). As a result, union members on an investment committee tend to have a shorter-term time horizon so that they can demonstrate to their union members that they have had an impact on actions taken. Meanwhile, corporate management has a longer-term view as dictated by the promises they have made. The differences in the time horizon between the two parties almost guarantees that performance will be negatively affected.

- *Time allocation*: To be effective, committee members must put in the time and effort. Time is required not just for meetings, but also to prepare for each meeting—which is as important as the meeting itself. Some of the popular business books these days are about overall *governance*. The purpose of a pension or investment fund is to provide a living for people who are in retirement or will be moving into retirement. Plan sponsors are responsible for the ongoing administration and management of the pension or investment fund—managed for the sole benefit of the plan beneficiaries. This aim is very clear. Plan sponsors must find a way to fulfill their fiduciary responsibility by providing the time, effort, and resources needed to monitor and evaluate all investment activities.

- *Emotions*: Perhaps the greatest detrimental impact on longer-term performance from investment committee members has to do with placing too much weight on current events and recent past performance. Emotions can get in the way of good common sense. As we age, we tend to become less patient. Short-termism tends to dominate the decisions in the investment industry—as shown in the increase in securities turnover within investment portfolios at the manager level and the increase in investment manager turnover at the plan sponsor level. The gap has widened between the longevity of the pension and investment funds and the decisions made at the investment committee level.

In summary, in recent decades, it has become significantly more complicated to administer the activities of a pension or investment fund. The investment committee is coming under increasing scrutiny and lawsuits seem to have become more prevalent. Thus, investment committees require more in-depth investment expertise and knowledge. The members need to take a longer-term view, delegate certain responsibilities as required, and resist the temptation to act on emotions caused by recent events. Sometimes doing nothing is the right decision.

PERFORMANCE INHIBITOR #6: ANALYSIS PARALYSIS

Just because something can be measured does not necessarily mean that the information gleaned from in-depth analysis is meaningful or useful in evaluating the investment management structure and the money managers within it. The plan sponsor spends significant amounts of time and effort to determine the appropriate risk tolerance and appetite, formulate the right asset mix, select best-in-show managers, track portfolio characteristics, and dissect performance results at the asset mix level, the asset class level, and the money manager level. Performance attribution allocates above-average and below-average performance into smaller and smaller segments (e.g., country impact, sector weighting, security selection, cash effect, market impact, and timing—with a small percentage left over for when the portfolio manager took a lunch break and left the portfolio unattended).

We now have the information ratio, Sharpe ratio, alpha, tracking error, and VaR—among other measures. Consultants and investment committee members use these data to evaluate the portfolio structure and overall performance. Most managers also track these statistics—not necessarily because they manage to these statistics, but because they want to know what the consultants are showing the managers' clients so that they can explain in detail why most of these statistics don't matter. If the managers don't use these statistics to construct portfolios, and the portfolios are always evaluated after the fact, then most of these statistics are not likely to assist the plan sponsor in understanding the decision-making process. However, some statistics are useful when tracking portfolio characteristics to ensure that managers stay within their style box. In addition, some information can determine whether bets are getting smaller, which could negatively impact future value-added results.

Most of the statistics being calculated have the overriding flaw of assuming that the benchmark being used for measurement purposes is representative of the manager's investment style, decision-making process, and investment approach. In fact, this is a major leap of faith. If the specific benchmark or index is suspect (for further details, refer to Chapter Six: When Performance Measurement Goes Awry), then every ratio, statistic, and analysis calculated against this benchmark/index must be suspect.

The solution is to be selective in what is measured. The information gathered should be useful for evaluating the decisions made at the policy level, the strategy currently in place, and the effective monitoring of portfolio characteristics and performance at the manager level. Again, reliance on specific ratios could send the wrong message to the plan sponsor's money managers. For example, one mixed signal may be derived from *tracking error.* Tracking error is defined as a measure of a manager's volatility against the benchmark. It records "relative risk". The lower the tracking error, the more index-like the portfolio. Consultants tend to give a manager a relatively high value-added performance target against the benchmark, while restricting the manager to a relatively low tracking error. This is inconsistent, as the manager's performance objective is to outperform the market, yet they cannot do so by looking a lot like the market. The fact that this statistic has the word "error" in it should offer some clue as to its effectiveness.

In summary, if a manager does not use a specific statistic in constructing its portfolio, or the manager states that a statistic is not relevant, then that statistic might not assist the investment committee members with the information and insight needed to assess the effectiveness of a money manager. Only statistics that provide useful insights and understanding into a money manager's decision-making process should be tracked (e.g., performance over various time periods and portfolio characteristics).

PERFORMANCE INHIBITOR #7: QUESTIONABLE ACADEMIC STUDIES

The main debate for academics is whether investing is an *art* or a *science*. Active money managers believe that their trade is an art—that data become information, that information transforms into education, that education develops into knowledge, and that knowledge results in informed decisions that create value for plan sponsors, based on the manager's own beliefs, investment style, and approach. Passive approaches are provided by organizations that believe that markets are efficient and that any information about a company is already embedded in the price of the stock—these are the so-called *alpha-challenged* managers. Academics, meanwhile, focus mainly on the belief that investing is a science. They either believe that a) all the variables within the marketplace can be presented as mathematic formulas that can provide the money manager with an edge to provide above-average performance by exploiting market inefficiencies, or b) markets are efficient and, therefore, active approaches to outperform the market are non-existent.

In summary, the problem with academic research is that it can tilt investment policy away from the longer-term timeframe based on short-term wins.

The assumptions of academic studies based on short-term and limited data of samples, averages, and models can prove misleading. It is best to always question this research.

SUMMARY

The good news is that there are ways to eliminate the seven performance inhibitors identified in this chapter, or, at least, to reduce their impact significantly. When designing *investment guidelines*, the investment committee should ensure that they reflect its longer-term goals and objectives, as outlined in the investment policy statement. The guidelines should provide an effective link between the policy at the plan sponsor level and strategy at the manager level. Restrictive guidelines could affect how portfolios are constructed, which may be detrimental to the overall fund results.

A key takeaway is that the plan should not *over-diversify*. The quest for ultimate risk reduction could have a greater negative impact on performance than the benefit of lowering overall volatility. Risk management can largely be contained by the plan sponsor at the policy level (e.g., asset class selection and allocation, geographic distribution, term structure, and investment styles and managers). Too much diversification beyond this level may be counter-productive. Plan sponsors are the risk managers, while money managers should be the return seekers or risk takers.

Time should be aligned among the various players within the fund's investment program. A focus on short-term performance results at the manager level may cause unnecessary turnover at a significant cost to the total fund. Short-term imperfections do not appear to be as significant over the longer term.

The investment community has created a language of its own. It does so to keep people confused and in the dark (in the hope that plan sponsors won't realize that most of the talk is all smoke and mirrors—and that most professionals within the investment community don't really understand the jargon either). Effective *communication* is required. Plan sponsors and investment committee members must have the in-depth experience and investment knowledge to understand the advice they receive from consultants and the decision-making process of the money managers.

There is no substitute for *experienced investment professionals* on an investment committee. The focus must be on the longer-term benefit of all plan participants. Committee members should use whatever resources are needed to fulfill their fiduciary responsibilities. Members must not over-react to recent events or get caught up in the latest fads. Another requirement is that investment committee members should ensure they have the *time* needed to act as a watchdog over all investment activities.

It is important to gather only *statistics* that will assist the investment committee in evaluating the aspects of the investment activities that can and should be measured—that is, to aid their oversight role and required actions. Too much data can distract from meaningful information. The investment committee should know what has to be measured, how it is going to be measured, how it is going to be reported, how it will be evaluated, and how it will impact their decision-making process going forward.

Finally, *academic studies* are precisely that—academic. Often, the research may not reflect reality. Just because something works well in one country, or in a segment of the market, or within a specific time period, does not mean it will work in other countries, or other areas of the marketplace, or in another time period.

Bottom line: These seven performance inhibitors do not have to come into play. Investment guidelines do not have to be restrictive. Diversification can be controlled at the total fund level, allowing greater opportunity for return enhancement at the investment management level. Any mismatch in time can be addressed by better understanding the focus of each service provider. Communication between the three parties (plan sponsor, money manager, and consultant/actuary) can be effective if worked on at the beginning of the relationship by outlining what each party brings to the table. Investment committees can become more productive with members who have investment-related experience and focus on what is important in their fiduciary role.

CHAPTER FOUR

GAMING AGAINST YOU

Not Everyone Is Your Friend

Just a thought:

I am not one for rules, however, this past summer, at the beach, it became painfully obvious that someone should put an age and weight restriction on men and their Speedos.

INTRODUCTION

The pension industry in North America, as we know it today, had its beginnings in the 1950s. Since then, the industry has shown explosive growth. This growth in investable assets has also occurred in institutional-type funds, operating and endowment funds, charitable organizations, foundations, insurance funds, and mutual funds, as well as pools of monies for private wealth (the affluent), and has attracted the attention of many service providers seeking to participate in this growth. According to the Organisation for Economic Co-operation and Development (OECD), the U.S. pension fund market in 2018 was about U.S. $15.6 trillion (with the U.S. ranking first in the world by size of pension assets), while Canada's pension fund market was about U.S. $1.5 trillion (with Canada ranking fourth in the world).

Figure 4.1 below highlights the various service providers and other interest groups that support the pension and other investment type funds—to varying degrees.

FIGURE 4.1: THE PLAYERS

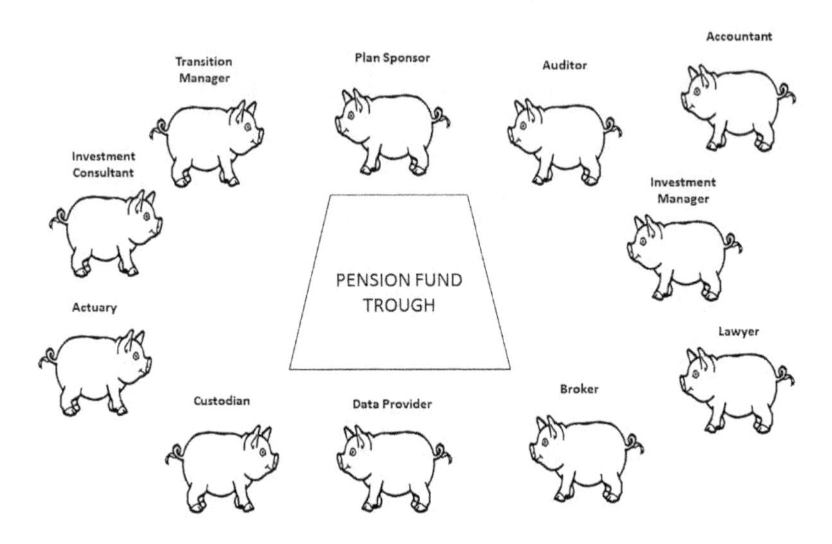

With most professions (e.g., accounting, law, teaching, and medicine), there are good professionals and there are bad ones—the few who may take advantage of their positions for their own financial benefit, gains, and self-interest. However, there really is no industry quite like the investment management industry when it comes to the potential of rewarding unethical behavior. The financial benefits to investment professionals or organizations of pushing the envelope a little further can run into the tens of millions of dollars. The investment industry likely has more conflicts of interest between those administering the funds for the benefit of their beneficiaries and those in a servicing capacity for the assets managed.

I acknowledge that my comments sound pretty dire and, perhaps, somewhat cynical. By and large, the pension and investment fields and the service providers supporting them operate with a high degree of integrity, honesty, prudence, and trustworthiness. However, several potential conflicts of interest exist and have been breached at one time or another. The purpose of this chapter is to outline conflicts and the potential conflicts of interest that the various service providers have in interacting with pension and investment funds. As well, there are some services (although, perhaps, not within the normal definition of "conflict of interest") where plan sponsors might be at a disadvantage given the specific nature of the service or product offered—not really getting the value they paid for. This will allow investment committee members to form their own judgments as to whether these conflicts or potential conflicts of interest could or would negatively affect the ongoing function of the investment program.

The conflicts of interest that arise for some of the various service providers are discussed in the following sections.

THE TIME-KEEPERS

Professionals within certain fields (e.g., accountants, actuaries, auditors, investment planning consultants, and lawyers) may primarily support pension and investment fund activities by charging for their services hourly. When dealing with clients, these professionals tend to keep "time sheets" that track the amount of time spent on each project. For some professionals within these fields, the path to partnership or advancement is primarily based on the revenues they generate, the number of client relationships they have, and the pedigree of their client base. As a result, there is a built-in incentive for these professionals to charge as much as the market will bear for any project undertaken, as well as to promote more projects that might not necessarily be of benefit to their clients. The *compensation philosophy and structure* of these firms represents a potential conflict of interest with their pension and investment fund clients.

Plan sponsors should always ask their outside relationships how fees are determined for any project or service undertaken. The costs of most projects are negotiable—and it is one of the responsibilities of the fiduciary to control overall costs. In addition, plan sponsors need to ensure that the projects undertaken are worth the time, effort, and cost, providing the information or education required to make informed judgments. Most projects should be put out to tender, even if the plan sponsor has an ongoing relationship with one of the service providers.

Actuarial and Consulting Services

There are several activities that may result in conflicts of interest for investment planning consulting firms and actuarial firms, as shown below:

- *Service versus product versus advice*: Up until the 1990s, investment planning consulting firms and actuarial firms had been mostly purists—providing only a "service" to the pension and investment community that covered a fairly wide range of activities (e.g., undertaking asset/liability studies, assisting in formulating asset mix policy, designing investment management structures, undertaking investment manager and custodial searches, and providing performance measurement comparisons and analytics).

  From the 1990s on, a number of consulting organizations began to expand their business models by offering a range of investment-related products and services to plan sponsors—the most recent one being the "bundled" investment manager platform. This platform would include equity managers (e.g., domestic plus non-domestic and, perhaps, managers with investment style offsets), fixed-income managers (e.g., a long-duration manager and a corporate-only manager), a real estate manager, and, if the fund were large enough, managers that fit in the alternative asset category (e.g., private equity, hedge funds, and infrastructure).

  With this package, there is generally a single set fee arrangement that includes the aggregate money management fees for all the investment managers within the structure as well as the fee for the consulting organization in overseeing the program. With this product structure, these consulting organizations now act as both a money management organization, managing the money management structure for clients, and a consulting organization, giving advice. For example, the plan sponsor could approach the consulting firm to undertake a money manager search only to have the consulting firm turn around and recommend its own investment management platform. This might not be in the best interest of the client, although it is definitely in the best financial interest of the consulting organization—which trades a short-term project fee from a one-off manager search for a longer-term continuous revenue stream generated by the money management platform. It is no secret that the money management side is more lucrative than the consulting side. As a result, some consulting firms have moved completely away from providing consulting services to focus exclusively on marketing their investment management platforms. A consulting firm that provides both an investment management platform and a consulting service has lost its objectivity.

- *Unnecessary money manager turnover*: For performance measurement consultants, 25% of all the money managers within their peer-group surveys fall within the fourth quartile (their selection pool for recommending manager turnover)—a self-generating revenue source. Manager turnover by the consulting firms is a revenue-generating activity. It is important to know if money managers are being terminated for the right reasons—not just because in one specific time period the manager placed in the fourth quartile and missed the value-added target by a smidgen. Manager turnover for the plan sponsor is expensive, involving the cost of the search by the consulting firm, the time and effort of the investment committee members, and the transactional cost when the portfolio moves from one manager to another.

- *Inexperienced analysts*: In the majority of investment consulting firms the research analysts evaluating, ranking, and monitoring the money management community are relatively young (read, inexperienced). This results in analysts with, perhaps, 5 to 10 years of only consulting experience (and not necessarily hands-on, investment-related experience) evaluating and ranking money managers with 30 to 40 years of pure investment-related experience. In most consulting organizations, the role of a research analyst is a stepping-stone to the position of a consultant, with direct client relationships, before making the ultimate move to partnership. It is frustrating for money managers to see the turnover of research analysts within consulting firms, particularly when one of the first questions these analysts ask money managers is how stable their money management team has been. It is ironic that most of these analysts and investment planning consultants wish to be money managers—they just have not figured out how to get there. As a result, plan sponsors might not be getting the most appropriate money managers for the mandates they have chosen. Evaluating money managers is a unique skill and requires in-depth expertise in understanding a money manager's beliefs, decision-making process, and value-added skills, and, most importantly, in how to "judge" the quality of the investment professionals. If not ranked the very best possible, managers might be hired who are not the right fit for the plan sponsor.

- *Money manager favorites*: Not all money managers are created equal. Consultants, after many meetings with money managers and money management organizations, and checking all the boxes on both a quantitative and qualitative basis, rank managers as a "strong buy", a "buy", a "hold", "on watch", or a "sell"—or some similar type of rating system. However, even within the same consulting organization, one consultant may put together a short list of candidates for a manager search for a plan sponsor that is different from the list another consultant within the same organization would choose for their client for the same mandate. In addition, the rating of a manager could change if there were a change within the consulting organization in the money manager's coverage, even with no changes in the money management organization itself—if that research analyst had different ranking criteria. Personalities can come into play here. Thus, the potential conflict of interest arises when the investment committee members do not know whether the list of managers it is given to select from is the most appropriate one from that specific consulting organization. Plan sponsors should ask how money managers are evaluated and rated, by whom, and what criteria is used for rating these managers.

- *Lack of manager coverage*: Not all consulting organizations have the supportive staff depth or the experience to cover all the money managers around the world. Some 30 or 40 years ago, with fewer money management organizations, managers were mainly judged on a qualitative basis. Now, due to the vast number of managers with many more investment mandates, and with more non-traditional asset classes, managers are rated more on a quantitative basis—with fewer face-to-face meetings. This shift is also a result of having to fulfill billable-hour requirements for consulting firms—as undertaking manager interviews (a non-paying activity) reduces time spent on client-related paying activities. The investment committee members will want to know if the consulting firm has dedicated full-time analysts to cover the money management community, how they are compensated, and the average age and experience level of the team.

- *Peer-group samples*: Some consulting firms gather performance data from plan sponsors and money management organizations to create "samples" for specific mandates (based on asset classes, asset class segments, investment styles, investment approaches, etc.). Some peer-group samples are created exclusively from data from the actual plan sponsors, while other samples are created exclusively from the money management community. The makeup and approach to sample construction may differ from one consulting or measurement service to another. Some samples may include exclusively commingled funds, while others may include only segregated portfolios. Commingled funds and segregated portfolios are not comparable and should not be in the same sample (e.g., commingled funds have internal costs that may not be included within segregated portfolios). Furthermore, money managers may be able to select the portfolios that will be included in the samples (this is an obvious advantage to the money manager, as it can select portfolios with the best performance history). Thus, peer-group samples from the various consulting and performance measurement firms are not likely to be identical. The potential concern arises when within one peer-group sample, a manager's performance for a portfolio places in the second quartile, while within another peer-group sample from another consultant, the manager's performance for the same fund places in the third quartile. One consultant does not include this manager in a search while the other one does. For peer-group samples, given the different methodology in constructing the samples, several biases creep in. It is important to know how samples are constructed and where and how the portfolio returns are generated.

Refer to Chapter Six, When Performance Measurement Goes Awry, for further details on peer-group sampling.

- *Monitoring overkill*: Consulting firms have basically positioned themselves to provide a monitoring and evaluation service to plan sponsors. The more complicated the investment management structure they create, and the more managers they typically can place within this structure, the higher the monitoring fees, and the more dependent the plan sponsor becomes on the consulting organization. There is a strong incentive for consulting firms to make themselves indispensable.

- *Money management services*: Some consulting firms provide money management services to money managers for a fee. For the majority of investment manager searches, the consultant is the intermediary—providing a short list of money manager candidates to their clients. Money managers may feel obligated to purchase a consulting firm's money management services (regardless of whether the service is necessary to the manager's decision-making process), as they fear being excluded from the consulting firm's search activities. This is a significant conflict of interest when the consulting firm has a revenue source from both the plan sponsor community and the money management industry—will the consulting firms feel obligated to place a money manager paying for their money management services on a mandate short list?

- *Outsourcing*: Over the past decade or so, some consulting firms have taken on the role of providing an outsourced chief investment officer function (as discussed under the heading "Service versus product versus advice" earlier in this section for plan sponsors). The consulting firm may provide a complete bundled service that includes some or all of the functions involved in managing and evaluating ongoing pension and investment fund activities (e.g., asset/liability studies; asset class selection and weighting; hiring investment managers to manage the various asset classes and asset class segments; and performance measurement). The potential conflict of interest lies in the consulting organization's selection of the various service providers for the platform. Not all managers are willing to participate in these platforms, and the program might therefore not include the best-of-the-best. Furthermore, since the platform is a revenue-generating source for the consulting organization, managers may be chosen based on how much they are willing to reduce their money management fees. Also, a manager termination may be slow to materialize, as undertaking the search would result in a hard-dollar cost to the organization, the market impact may negatively affect overall performance and, perhaps, show clients that the consulting organization made an error in hiring the manager in the first place.

Outside of the money management firm, the consulting community has the most potential conflicts of interest. The partners of these consulting organizations have a strong incentive to focus on the bottom line—perhaps, at the expense of the plan sponsor.

Accountants, Auditors, and Lawyers

As with consultants and actuaries, accountants, auditors, and lawyers have billable hours as their main compensation philosophy for internal staff promotions and succession. As a result, the following conflicts of interest may arise:

- *Promoting other services*: As with the other time-keepers, these firms have a strong incentive to promote other services that they offer. The goal is always to get as many tentacles around the client as possible; however, not all of these services may be necessary or useful to the plan sponsor.

- *Increasing fees*: It seems that their fees for service tend to increase at a rate significantly higher than the rate of inflation on a yearly basis. Although not a conflict of interest, this is a cost that may be borne by the investment fund. One recourse is to let these service providers know that their services will be put out to tender every two or three years.

When quoted any fee for a service, ask the service providers how the fees are determined. Ask for details. It is the committee's fiduciary responsibility to understand what it is paying for.

PLAN SPONSOR

The plan sponsor might also have potential conflicts of interest in administering and managing the investment funds for its participants and their beneficiaries, as shown in the following point:

- *Pension versus corporate priorities*: A defined-benefit pension fund within a corporation competes for funds with their other business lines. If pension fund returns are above expectations, resulting in a fund surplus, the corporation is likely not required to put in additional monies beyond what had been anticipated. If longer-term performance is below expectations (the more likely scenario due to market fluctuations) and the fund moves into a deficit position, the corporation might have to ante up more monies to shore up the pension fund. The balancing act for the plan sponsor is to achieve the highest return possible on the fund without creating so much volatility that could require an infusion of capital. Changes in accounting practices in the last three decades have placed the volatility of the fund on the earnings statement and the liability on the balance sheet; thus, corporate priorities may prove to be in conflict with pension priorities.

The plan sponsor must ensure that the fund assets are managed exclusively for the plan members and their beneficiaries. The priorities must be aligned.

THE EXECUTIONERS

Brokerage firms are responsible for implementing and executing buy and sell transactions for their clients (basically, the money managers). For this service, brokerage firms extract a commission fee for these transactions that is typically quoted in cents per share. As an example, if 100,000 shares were traded in a relatively liquid security, the cost per share might be 3 to 4 cents. For a full-service brokerage firm, this fee covers the cost of pure execution (close to 1 cent per share), proprietary and third-party research, and servicing and coverage (the remainder). Potential conflicts of interest with the brokerage community are as follows:

- *Investor prioritization*: Here, size matters. It is no surprise that brokerage firms rank their clients by the amount of commissions they generate. The scale is easy: the money managers with the largest commission pools are ranked number one (or A), the next level of commission generators is ranked number two (or B), and the third level (those with the lowest amount of commission dollars) is ranked number three (or C). Each level has a different service proposition—with the managers ranked the highest getting the most in-depth service coverage. Most importantly, they typically get "first call" when new ideas or recommendations are produced by the brokerage firm's research team—and are called first when trades become available. Smaller firms are at a disadvantage here. In recent decades, money management firms have tended to spend more time and money producing their own internal research and, by doing so, are increasingly seeking out discount brokers and trading on an "execution-only" basis. Trading costs are a cost of implementing portfolio strategy.

- *Soft dollars/directed commissions*: Money managers that have soft-dollar commitments or directed commission arrangements on behalf of their clients may find themselves at a disadvantage when trading. First, not all brokerage firms accept soft-dollar transactions—as a result, soft-dollar trades might be allocated to other brokerage firms that might not have as an effective trading desk in place (not fulfilling the "best execution" objective). Second, if soft-dollar/directed commission trades cannot be commingled with other trades, the client might miss out on attractive trade opportunities (as their soft-dollar trades would be executed after the main trade is completed for other clients that do not have these arrangements). For brokerage firms that permit some soft-dollar trades, the trading desk might call these clients last, if they know that part of the commission dollar will leave the trading desk's commission pool and be directed somewhere else within the brokerage firm. To counteract this, managers might not tell the trading desk that it is a soft-dollar trade until after the trade is complete; however, the broker's trading desk generally knows which managers have soft-dollar arrangements and might still not call these clients first—just in case the next trade is for their soft-dollar arrangements.

Refer to Chapter Seven, Trade Commission Dollars, for further information on soft-dollar trades and directed commission arrangements.

- *Commission charges*: The per-share cost of commissions has been cut by about half since the early 1980s. As a result, brokerage firms have become more competitive in their service capabilities, execution efficiencies, and research offerings (both proprietary and what they arrange with third-party vendors). However, in the vast majority of brokerage firms (discount brokerage firms being the exception), the commission rate quoted is bundled, obscuring the real cost of execution and the residual (the overall cost of research and servicing from one brokerage firm to another). This lack of transparency makes it difficult for the plan sponsor to determine the actual cost of administering and managing the investment fund.

Brokerage firms have a number of potential conflicts. Unfortunately, it is very difficult to judge the overall cost to the investment fund. There is a lot of trust placed in money managers to achieve "best execution."

KEEPERS OF THE CRYPT

Custodians are not as visible a service and, as a result, they may not receive as much attention as they should in the monitoring and evaluation process. However, conflicts of interest may arise for custodians as outlined below:

- *Security lending*: No matter how sophisticated the investment community becomes, there is always some slippage between when securities are *expected* to be delivered to the new owner after purchase, and when they are *actually* delivered—this delivery delay is typically measured in days. However, in special circumstances, it is not uncommon for security delivery to be delayed by weeks. As a result, there is a need for a security inventory from which securities may be lent so they can be delivered on time. This is where the custodians come in—given that the shares owned by their clients are sitting in their vaults collecting dust. This provides an economic benefit to plan sponsors for their securities held in safekeeping by the custodian—due to these inefficiencies within the trading system. Custodians, with permission from their clients, may lend out securities for a fee to fill this time-delay gap. To reduce the risk exposure to the client, the custodian puts up collateral (typically, Treasury Bills). The fee arrangement for security lending between the custodian and the client is generally on some percentage split between the plan sponsor and the custodian. A conflict might arise if one client offers a better percentage split than another client in favor of the custodian, or if the client is a major client of the bank or trust company with the lender going right to the top of the queue. If investment committee members develop a securities lending program, they should know the selection priority process of their custodian. Security lending might be one of those "free lunches" for plan sponsors—as there is an income stream with very little risk.

- *Transaction costs*: Custodians charge a fee for every trade undertaken by the money managers for their clients. This fee varies between stocks traded in North America (relatively low fees per trade), other developed markets (slightly higher fees), and less developed markets of the world (much higher fees). These costs tend to be hidden to the plan sponsor and can significantly add up if investment funds have an emerging market component, or if managers have high turnover rates within their non-domestic portfolios. Again, without full transparency, it is difficult to know the overall cost of administering and managing an investment program.

- *Currency conversion*: This area can result in a major conflict of interest with the plan sponsor. Currency conversions from one country to another can be manipulated by the custodian (and the brokerage firm) based on the time of day when the conversion trigger takes place. Currencies fluctuate and can produce fairly wide swings during the day, which can result in a significant cost to the portfolio—and a potential gain for the custodian (and/or the brokerage firm). This is truly one of the hidden costs of doing business and can end up being very costly to the fund, as the timing during the day for conversion may be at the discretion of the custodian or brokerage firm. Again, full monitoring and transparency are required.

Investment committee members must take the time to evaluate the activities of their custodians. Most investment committees take this part of the investment program for granted. Once again, this is a cost of doing business and the fiduciary responsibility of the investment committee.

INVESTMENT COMMITTEES

As stated often, the investment committee has the fiduciary responsibility to ensure that pension and investment funds are administered and managed in an effective and efficient manner for the sole benefit of the plan participants and their beneficiaries. The following areas may present the investment committee members with conflicts of interest, risks, and challenges with these stated goals:

- *Inexperienced members*: A consistent theme throughout this book is that investment committee members should have some background and experience in most investment-related matters. Even having an experienced investment professional as an outside consultant may not be enough if committee members do not have the required knowledge to ask the right questions. This lack of education and experience is likely the greatest risk to the investment fund not achieving its goals and objectives. It is important for all committee members to understand the nuances of the investment management community. Committee members who do not have the required experience must ensure they have access to the education, knowledge, and experience of experts to fulfill their fiduciary responsibility—and know when to ask for it, where to get it, and when to use it.

- *Short-term focus*: The vast majority of pension and investment funds have a relatively long-term time horizon before funds are required for liquidation. This provides an opportunity for the investment committee to take a longer-term time perspective when formulating asset mix policy and strategy. Committee members can get sidetracked by short-term events. Any short-term adjustment, based on market movements or market expectations, to the longer-term asset mix policy is considered market timing—and there are few, if any, studies that have conclusively demonstrated that market timing adds value to the longer-term rate of return of an investment fund (in fact, the vast majority of academic studies say just the opposite—that the cost of market timing actually detracts from longer-term returns). Committee members must match the decisions they make to the longer-term timeframe of the fund.

- *Lack of time commitment*: Administering and managing the investment platform for a pension or investment fund is time consuming (at least, it should be). The same amount of time and effort that goes into other divisions of an organization should also go into managing all the activities of the investment program. If the necessary time is not allocated to this undertaking, it could have a significant detrimental impact on the longer-term rate of return—no matter how experienced the members. As mentioned before, being a member of an investment committee is not a part-time undertaking.

- *Moving too fast or too slow*: The various activities of managing the investment fund must be monitored and evaluated, and steps must be taken when things go off track. Termination of a money manager should be triggered only after careful consideration by the investment committee members. Moving too fast could result in costly manager turnover and might not work out as anticipated (as the newly hired manager with first-quartile performance might not live up to short-term expectations—perhaps due to hiring the manager at its peak performance). However, if the circumstances within the money management firm have changed from when the manager was hired (e.g., ownership change, personnel changes, and style or process changes), moving too slow could be detrimental to long-term results. It is a true balancing act.

- *Lack of accountability*: The plan sponsor and the investment committee are responsible for a number of activities—as outlined in Chapter One and Chapter Two. The decisions the investment committee makes should be monitored to determine success (or, perhaps, failure)—events that may provide a learning opportunity. The people or teams with certain responsibilities and authority should know that the decisions they make will be assessed and evaluated—there is no greater incentive for a person to focus on the task at hand than knowing they will be judged on their decisions. There is no "participation ribbon" here. Committee members must learn from their mistakes—and, yes, there will be mistakes.

- *Multi-employer plans*: Most investment committees of multi-employer pension and investment funds have a built-in conflict of interest. In general, the management team focuses on the longer-term nature of the fund, with an emphasis on attempting to ensure that the plan sponsor does not have to allocate any more monies to the investment fund than what has been determined already. Union members typically have a shorter-term focus, as one of their goals is to get re-elected; as indicated earlier in the chapter, there are perks associated with being an investment committee member, given that investment conferences are generally held in exotic locations, and committee members have the opportunity to visit money managers in other countries.

- *Personal conflicts of interest*: It goes without saying that all investment committee members should eliminate, or reduce as best possible, any conflicts of interest or potential conflicts of interest. Conflicts of interest arise when an activity associated with the investment fund results in a financial reward or other type of benefit that accrues to an individual or investment committee member. In addition, members might have affiliations with outside service providers that could lead to a potential conflict of interest if the relationship would result in a benefit to the member. Investment committee members should not accept gifts or trips paid for by any existing service provider or potential service provider—anything that could create a situation that might favor one firm over another. In the investment industry, decisions are judged on perception. Nothing should ever look suspicious.

  Refer to Appendix 1 for a sample policy that includes a reference to conflicts of interest.

- *Biases*: With the trend toward globalization and alternative asset classes within the money management community, the number of managers that the plan sponsor can choose from has increased significantly. One of the perks of being on an investment committee is being able to visit managers (part of the due-diligence process) in their natural habitat (for non-domestic managers, places like London, Tokyo, Hong Kong, and Paris). Given the trend to global investment mandates, there is a temptation to select managers due to their head office location. In addition, committee members who serve on more than one investment committee may have manager favorites. Just because the manager worked out well for one client does not mean that the same would happen with another client—especially if the mandate is slightly different. Also, do not confuse a money manager's ability to manage a private wealth portfolio for an investment committee member with the manager's ability to manage an institutional-type portfolio for the plan sponsor.

Investment committee members must gather the resources needed to fulfill their fiduciary responsibilities. They must eliminate any conflicts that would negatively affect their role.

INVESTMENT MANAGERS

Most conflicts and potential conflicts of interest come from the money management community. The list is fairly extensive. Having worked within two money management firms, as well as two investment planning consulting firms, I have found that even money management firms don't completely understand or recognize all the conflicts of interest associated with managing money for their clients. Some of these conflicts of interest just go unobserved—occurring without their knowledge. While a money manager's failure to recognize a conflict of interest in how it manages money for clients is not a valid excuse, remember that the main focus of these firms is on investment management, marketing, and servicing (although in some money management firms, the first two activities could be reversed in order of priority). For money managers, very little time is spent on building an infrastructure that focuses on eliminating or reducing any conflicts of interest with clients—after all, to do so would be a cost to the organization.

Some potential conflicts of interest are highlighted below:

- *Client type*: There are three primary client types that seek out money management expertise: 1) *institutional-oriented clients* (e.g., pension funds, insurance accounts, operating and endowment funds, and foundations); 2) *private wealth clients* (basically, high net worth individuals with over $1 million in total investable assets); and 3) *retail clients* (typically, individuals with less than $1 million in investable assets who may use financial planners and/or advisors for investment advice). Money management firms typically provide investment management support to one, two, or all three of these client types. These three client types typically have different risk parameters, time horizons, and return objectives. For institutional accounts, selecting a money management firm is based primarily on the stability of the firm, how long it has been in business, the quality and depth of the investment professional teams, the decision-making process, investment style and approach, and ownership structure. For individual investors using mutual funds, the main selection criteria center around performance (basically, short-term performance). For private wealth investors, the selection criteria lie somewhere between what institutions look for and what mutual fund clients look for. In some of the smaller money management firms, the investment management team may manage the investment funds for two or all three of these investment client types. For the larger firms, there may be a separate team managing the assets for each of these three client types. Either way, the question is, which client type is most important to the money management organization? This question becomes pertinent when there is a new research idea that is perceived to be very attractive; however, the stock is somewhat illiquid and will not fill the target weighting of all three client types. Where do the priorities lie?

Conflicts of interest arise due to the management fees related to each of these three client types. Mutual funds and wrap programs (a platform offered by the brokerage community for their individual clients) are associated with the highest management fees—followed by fees for private wealth investors. Fees for institutions are at the lower end of the scale. The incentives tilt away from pension and institutional-type investment funds toward those of the money managers' individual clients. This is perhaps the greatest of all the conflicts of interest associated with money management firms. If a money management organization services more than one of these client types, there should be separate accountability for each client-type channel.

In addition, some clients may get a fee break based on who they are (e.g., religious organizations and charitable foundations). Although I have empathy for these organizations, I do not believe that money management firms should give any of their clients special fee arrangements (typically, reducing their posted fee schedule by, say, 10%). This is favoring one client type over another—no matter how great the cause.

- *Soft dollars*: Money management firms may use the commission dollars of their clients to pay for research (both proprietary and third-party), as well as equipment, databases, and measurement services used by the money managers. Any service purchased with commission dollars *must* be linked into the money manager's investment decision-making process. The following questions must be asked: 1) Do all the services paid for by soft dollars relate directly in the manager's decision-making process for the plan sponsor? 2) Are all the services actually beneficial in reducing the risk of the investment fund or increasing the return? 3) Will these services reduce the cost of administering and managing the fund assets? The conflict of interest arises when there are services that are purchased on the periphery that might not make a difference to portfolio implementation one way or the other. If soft-dollar trades from the money manager were eliminated, would the manager be able to lower the trading costs by a cent or two—to the exclusive benefit to the plan sponsor (i.e., any reduction in execution costs goes right to the bottom line of the portfolio and, thus, enhances fund performance)? I strongly believe that only research should be paid for with soft dollars (all other services being paid would or should be a business expense of the money manager), and soft dollars should only be used for third-party research when that service cannot be paid for with hard dollars. This eliminates most of the potential conflicts of interest.

Refer to Chapter Seven, Trade Commission Dollars, for a more in-depth discussion on "soft dollars."

- *Client priorities*: Just as brokerage firms rank their clients by how much revenue or prestige they bring to the firm, money management organizations also rank their own clients. Clients are valued on the revenue stream they bring to the firm—or their pedigree. The top-tier clients are treated differently. They get the very best servicing professionals within the organization, visits from the senior portfolio managers, more investment review meetings, more invitations to special events, more lunches and dinners, and so on. The money manager should have a policy in place that outlines how the priorities with different clients are handled (e.g., how trades are allotted between the various client types and within a specific client type).

- *Compensation*: It is important to have a thorough understanding of the remuneration structure and incentives for the investment professionals on an individual, team, and company basis. Overall compensation should be aligned with the performance goals and objectives of the pension or investment fund. If the client's performance objectives are met or exceeded, the investment professionals *should* be rewarded accordingly—if the individual or team was responsible for this performance (i.e., skill, not luck). If performance falls below expectations, the client should not be the only one to suffer. Determining if historical performance was driven by skill is the most difficult assessment that a plan sponsor will make. Primarily, consider if the money manager is rewarded for the short-term performance of the portfolio, which might not align with the goals of the investment fund, or with longer-term incentives that align more closely with the objectives of the investment fund. A lot of faith goes into this decision.

- *Personal trading*: One of the potential conflicts of interest is the internal treatment of personal trades by investment professionals and designated staff for their own accounts (or accounts they have control over) within the money management organization. Some firms require pre-authorization from the compliance officer or the compliance department before investment professionals can make a trade for their own personal portfolio. If the request is for an issue that is currently on the trading desk for execution, or is expected to be on the desk shortly by conferring with the money management teams, then the personal trade generally would not be allowed until the trade process was completed for their clients. Another option is for the money management firm to set up a "partner fund" in which all personal employee investments are managed. It sounds like a good idea, but may create a conflict of interest when the investment professionals compete with their clients for issues. A third option is to permit investment professionals (or anyone that comes into contact with the trading slips) to invest only in the commingled funds managed by the firm (if commingled funds are available). The small benefit here is being able to tell clients that the investment professionals invest in the funds that their clients use and therefore have their performance objectives aligned with those of the clients. The investment committee members should ask the money manager for its policies on personal trading within the firm and how these personal trades are tracked.

- *Trade allocation*: Some of this topic overlaps with "client type"—the conflict of interest in which client channel receives the most attention. The potential conflict of interest comes when the money management organization has a significantly large asset base in one of its mandates and there are not enough shares available in an initial stock purchase for all client portfolios. This can occur quite often in smaller-cap mandates or portfolios that invest in less liquid areas of the markets. If the issue is fairly illiquid, it might take time to accumulate the desired position for each client's portfolio—and, as a result, the purchases would be at different times and at different prices. Money managers should have a trade allocation policy to deal with trade distributed among clients. Basically, the policy should specify how trades are prioritized.

- *Front-running*: This occurs when the money manager knows in advance that a large buy or sell order that could significantly move the price of the issue is about to be placed in the market, and puts their individual personal order in ahead of the larger order to gain an economic advantage. For example, an institutional-type client decides to sell a large order of a relatively illiquid stock. This sell order is likely to depress the price of the stock. The trader also owns some of this stock in their personal portfolio, which they decide to sell in the market before the larger sell order is known to the investing public. Once again, this generates a conflict of interest for the money management firm with its clients. Just because something is illegal doesn't mean that it can't or won't occur (it has happened in the past, and it will happen in the future).

- *Timing cash flows*: Investing in securities normally results in a fairly consistent and predictable cash flow from these securities within the portfolio—dividends from stocks and interest from bonds. These cash flows typically have to be reinvested. When to invest the cash flow becomes the potential conflict of interest. If a manager held back this cash flow and invested in securities in the last two days of the quarter, this might provide an artificial boost in performance. As a result, the manager with this higher performance might be attracting new clients. This is especially true for those mandates investing in the less liquid areas of the market. As a result, the performance history might be artificially inflated.

- *Performance presentations*: This is one area where money managers can game the system. When asked to present performance results to prospective clients, money managers have a slew of products, mandates, and portfolios to choose from—and are likely to pick their best-performing funds. They can also present performance data over specific time periods that show their best results. Money managers have become quite imaginative when it comes to presenting performance data and performance analytics. When conducting a search for a new manager, the consultant should present the performance results over various time periods with "composites" (a process where all the clients within a certain mandate are combined into one fund to show the weighted average return for all the clients' performance over time) on the various mandates and show the dispersion of performance results within these composites for the clients invested in the mandate. Actually, the consultant should also show the results in the worst possible light. If the money manager still looks attractive, the manager may be hired. Each manager should present their performance in the same way—with the consultant guaranteeing the performance data of all managers. For money management firms, CFA Institute has outlined performance reporting standards when presenting performance data to clients and prospects. Plan sponsors should ensure that managers are adhering to these standards.

- *Investment management fees*: For money management firms, there is typically a "posted" fee schedule based on a sliding fee scale for assets under management. Plan sponsors with smaller assets to manage pay a management fee at the higher end of the posted fee schedule, while plan sponsors with a much higher asset base pay management fees at the lower end of the scale. However, the posted rates like speed limit signs—and treated more like a guideline rather than a hard-and-fast rule. Moreover, within money management organizations, there is a financial incentive to offer products with the highest fees. Most money management firms, for clients and prospective clients with sizable assets to manage, may also offer a "negotiated fee" level—a shorter or a condensed version of the posted fee schedule, or, if large enough, one flat fee. The important issue here is not to pay more than another client in the same mandate with the approximate same asset base. A number of plan sponsors have introduced a "most-favored nation" clause within their money management agreements. This clause states that the plan sponsor does not pay more than another client with a similar mandate, with similar guidelines and performance standards, and similar asset size. For some firms, fees can be negotiated even for smaller accounts. The problem with most-favored nation clauses is that plan sponsors have to trust the manager to do the right thing by notifying them of a breach and enforcing the clause with future clients. Managers find it easy to prove why one client might be different to another.

- *Incentive-based fees*: Incentive-based fees can be initiated by the plan sponsor, the money management organization, or the investment planning consultant. Basically, an incentive-based fee is an *add-on fee* to the posted fee schedule and is triggered if the performance of the portfolio exceeds a pre-specified value-added target. If initiated by plan sponsors, they typically assume that the investment manager is not trying its hardest to deliver the very best performance possible. If the money management firm initiates an incentive-based fee structure, it suggests that the firm believes it can deliver more than the value-added target given by the plan sponsor, and wants a little more money for doing so. The conflict of interest arises when some clients have incentive-based fees while others do not. This creates a two-tiered system—with one group of clients having a, potentially, positive advantage over another. This creates self-interest on the manager's part. It is a similar issue to that raised earlier under "Client type," in which one client type may be favored over another due to one client type being more profitable than another. If there is a financial incentive that favors one client over another, it automatically creates a potential conflict of interest.

Refer to Chapter Eight, Incentive-based Fees, for a more in-depth discussion on incentive-based fees.

- *Insider trading*: Insider trading involves acting on confidential information that is not in the public realm and that may have an impact (positive or negative) on the price of the security. This is an illegal activity, by the way; however, it happens every now and then, and investors are fined and/or jailed. Once again, investment managers may have access to insider information through company contacts or friends within the brokerage community. Because of the financial benefit that can result in acting on insider information, it presents a temptation and, therefore, creates a potential conflict of interest.

- *Wrap programs*: As stated earlier in this chapter, wrap accounts are a bundled investment manager package offered mainly through brokerage firms. They include a blend of money managers that typically manage monies for institutional clients. The selling point here is that the *individual* clients of the brokerage firms have access to institutional-focused money managers—which these individuals would not be able to access directly due to their much lower asset base. The assumption is that institutional money managers are better at managing money than their retail counterparts (although I'm not sure that this is true). The money manager either manages the portfolios held within the wrap accounts or provides the brokerage firm with a model portfolio (the most likely scenario) on a predetermined basis, with the brokerage firm entering the trades through its retail trading desk. As with other situations in which there are diversified client types, conflicts of interest can arise in setting priorities, as wrap programs could be competing with the money manager at the same time that the money manager is in the marketplace for its institutional-type clients.

- *Asset growth*: One of the negative influences on longer-term performance is asset growth within a money management firm. As assets within a certain mandate grow, portfolio characteristics tend to change (e.g., the number of issues held in the portfolio increases, the dispersion around the various sectors and industries narrows, and the weighting in the top 10 names within the portfolio declines)—basically, the bets become smaller and smaller over time. As the bets become smaller, the ability to outperform the benchmark becomes more difficult. As a result, the historical value-added results might not be representative of what might be delivered in the future. Investment committee members should track these concentration bets to see if the asset growth in their specific mandate is changing due to the increasing asset base—which might have a negative impact on the value-added target in the future.

- *Errors and omissions*: Mistakes are made within money management organizations, brokerage firms, and at the custodian level. The manager might place an order to buy 10,000 shares of ABC Company. The brokerage firm might read this order as 100,000 shares. The shares are bought, yet the money is not available when the shares are delivered. The brokerage firm, whose mistake it was, has to sell the additional shares in the market—at a price that could be different from what the brokerage firm actually paid. This typically results in a loss to someone. If the manager makes a mistake, and there is a loss involved, the plan sponsor might not recognize or be aware if the cost of this mistake is somehow charged to its account. Plan sponsors must be aware that mistakes can happen and ensure that they are compensated for any mistakes by the responsible party.

As indicated earlier, a lot of trust is placed in investment managers to do all the right things.

In summary, potential conflicts of interest may arise between investing activities and many of the service providers for the investment fund. Although not all the issues outlined in this chapter are necessarily conflicts of interest, any issue that has the potential to reduce the overall return of the investment portfolio, increase the overall risk of the portfolio, or raise the overall cost of administering and managing the pension or investment program should be of concern to investment committee members.

The fiduciary responsibility of the plan sponsor is to eliminate or reduce as much as possible the chance of service providers gaming against the fund. These service providers act as agents on behalf of the plan sponsor and have certain responsibilities to fulfill their duties in a manner that reflects honesty, transparency, care, due diligence, and prudence. However, there is more temptation to deviate from what is right (and lawful) in the money management community than in most other professions, as the rewards are massive (if the perpetrator doesn't get caught). The most ingrained of all human characteristics are self-interest and self-preservation.

One way to mitigate the potential for conflicts of interest is to ensure that the necessary policies of the money management firms are well documented. In addition, the plan sponsor should obtain the conflict of interest policies of certain service providers and ask money managers how they ensure that one type of client is not favored over another type within their organizations.

Plan sponsors should ask their money managers, and any managers they are thinking of hiring, whether they record their interactions with the brokerage community and between their own money managers and their trading desk—and, if so, whether these conversations have ever been used to defend themselves or their clients, and what the outcome was. If a money manager is doing all the right things for its clients, recording conversations is a good way to protect both the money management firm and the client.

My experiences as a money manager, investment planning consultant, and plan sponsor have taught me that there are many very good service providers that fully operate in the best interests of their clients. I have no doubt of this. However, conflicts of interest and potential conflicts of interest are real—whether intentional or not and whether consciously or not. All of the conflicts of interest discussed in this chapter have been breached by some money managers or service providers at one time or another, or there would not be policies to address these issues. The points outlined in this chapter will, hopefully, assist investment committee members to enter relationships with service providers with eyes wide open. Preparation is everything. It puts the odds in the investment committee's favor.

CHAPTER FIVE

THE MANAGER SEARCH FOLLY

Not as Important as You May Think

Just a thought:

The definition of a money manager: an investment professional who manages your money until it is all gone.

INTRODUCTION

As outlined in Chapter One, plan sponsors have the fiduciary responsibility to act in the best interest of the plan beneficiaries—as a prudent person entrusted with investing the assets of others would. As a result, members of an investment committee must set up an appropriate platform to design and implement an investment program that effectively establishes policies and procedures to administer, supervise, manage, monitor, and control the fund assets. One of the investment committee's primary tasks is to select service providers, including money managers, who will follow the criteria outlined in the investment policy statement to deliver the performance objectives within the stated risk tolerance parameters.

Also as stated in Chapter One, the initial steps in this due-diligence process are as follows:

1. set out the *funding policy*;

2. create the *investment policy statement*, including the goals and objectives for the fund;

3. formulate an *asset mix policy* that includes the asset classes of choice, the policy weight, and tolerance ranges required to achieve the goals and objectives outlined in the funding policy;

4. it is best practice to include statements about the fund's *risk appetite*; and,

5. it is also best practice to provide statements on *investment beliefs*.

After completing or reviewing these five documents, the committee should be in a position to determine its approach to managing the fund's assets—which leads to the formulation of the investment management structure (e.g., terms, numbers, types, and allocation weights of investment mandates) to implement asset mix policy. It is now time to seek out professional investment managers to implement the investment mandates chosen.

The investment professionals within an organization provide the comfort for plan sponsors. Stability is necessary, as selecting a manager is, ideally, for the longer term. It is way too costly not to get it right the first time around. Plan sponsors should be looking for a partnership arrangement. There are too many other more important value-added issues for the investment committee to deal with than to spend time on manager searches every year or so. Excessive manager turnover might be the fault of the investment committee members—not lining up the appropriate resources to achieve the objectives laid out in the investment policy statement, a lack of in-depth investment expertise on the committee, and a strong tendency to pick the most recent winners. While there is some evidence of continued success of the "hot hand," it appears to evaporate usually after two or three years.

THE SELECTION PROCESS: THE BEGINNING

One of the most important and most challenging financial decisions made by investment committee members is choosing the most appropriate investment professionals, or investment management organizations, to deliver the desired result within the investment management structure. It should rather be thought of as selecting managers for their *most desirable fit for purpose*. What generally makes the manager selection process so difficult is the lack of experience and expertise of the investment committee members in understanding the investment community in-depth. It is not that the committee members are not intelligent, or at the top of their chosen profession; it is just that the majority are not trained or do not have the education, experience, and skills needed for selecting money managers. It is not their fault; it is just the way it is. Selecting money managers is a unique skill. The question always comes back to how investment committee members recognize the most desirable managers and organizations available for achieving the fund's goals and objectives, and aligning interests of the managers/organizations with those of the fund.

If the investment committee chooses to go the route of passive index-based strategies (which, in some cases, can be justified in part or even entirely), it rarely matters which of the major passive-driven organizations is selected. However, in choosing to hire active investment managers, the committee members must assess the manager's ability to generate above-average returns (or alpha) at an acceptable risk tolerance and acceptance level. To assess the likelihood of a manager's future success, the committee members must determine how a manager actually constructs and maintains a diversified portfolio of selected investments, at the appropriate risk level, and whether that organization and its investment process has what it takes to succeed in a competitive marketplace.

The manager evaluation process consists of two main parts. The first is a *qualitative* assessment. For example, have the investment committee members gained a sufficient understanding of the firm's vision, beliefs, values, investment decision-making process, and portfolio construction criteria? And, have the members assessed the education, experiences, and skills of the investment professionals responsible for portfolio implementation? The second part of the evaluation process is a *quantitative* assessment. For example, do the evidence portfolio characteristics confirm the manager's style and approach? Have the performance results provided historical evidence that the manager has delivered net value-added returns at an acceptable risk level against a predetermined, suitable benchmark or within an appropriate peer-group sample—in other words, delivering performance more through skill than luck?

Many studies have stated and confirmed that past performance results have low to zero predictive value in determining how a manager will perform in the future. If this is the case, the investment committee's emphasis on manager selection relies mainly on the qualitative assessment. However, as we know, people typically make decisions based on the presentation of hard facts (or what they perceive as facts). This results in managers being hired mainly on historical performance numbers, with fingers crossed. Here, there is a lot of implied emphasis on hope that the above-average performance is repeatable. Unfortunately, investment committee members too often rely heavily on the objective numbers to justify their decisions—despite the knowledge that "hard facts" really don't mean much, if anything at all. Judgment is necessarily subjective.

A lot has been written about quantitative assessment for selecting managers, since this topic is easier to address than qualitative assessment. The main focus of this chapter is on the qualitative assessment of evaluating and selecting the most desirable active managers, which, hopefully, will assist the investment committee members in understanding the complexities of engaging in a manager selection process, and increase the odds of selecting a superior manager to achieve the fund's overall goals.

Selecting the universe of managers for a specific mandate, culling the list to acceptable candidates, and then analyzing the qualitative and quantitative factors of each manager are all part of the due-diligence process.

SIX-STEP ASSESSMENT AND ENGAGEMENT PROCESS

The process for hiring and employing a money manager consists of six main steps:

> *Step 1) Setting Goals and Objectives:* Determining the specific goals and objectives of the fund needed to fulfill the committee's fiduciary responsibility to the beneficiaries of the plan;

Step 2) The Long List: Outlining the search criteria and procedures required to create a long list of potential candidates (usually between 8 and 12) to implement the overall strategic plan;

Step 3) The Lineup: Culling this list down to a short list of four to six managers and requesting proposals from these managers; meeting with these managers in their offices (or, at the very least, in the plan sponsor's offices); and then selecting two or three managers to give a final presentation to all committee members (if a manager selection team is established);

Step 4) Pick Me, Pick Me: Setting an interview agenda to gather as much pertinent information as possible for effective manager comparisons, and selecting the manager;

Step 5) Aligned Interests: Establishing the contractual conditions under which the chosen manager will operate; and,

Step 6) After the Ball: Creating a continuous monitoring and assessment process to assist in ensuring ongoing success.

Step 1: Setting Goals and Objectives

The manager selection process begins with formulating an investment policy statement. This statement must be effective, well documented, and custom designed to reflect the specific characteristics of the plan or fund. In today's environment, policy must be based on the specific promises that have been made to the beneficiaries, how risk is expressed, and how to provide a path from funding contributions and investment returns to making good on those promises.

Table 5.1 below shows the inputs required for an investment policy statement (one "theory" input on how the process should be, and one "reality" input on how things are in practice):

TABLE 5.1: INVESTMENT POLICY DESIGN MISMATCH

POLICY DESIGN	THEORY	REALITY
Plan Type/Funding/Promises	50–70%	15–35%
Business/Risk Appetite/Asset Size	30–40%	20–30%
Investment Committee Views	5–15%	50–60%

Although the plan characteristics and risk appetite should drive investment policy and the investment management structure, it is usually the specific attitudes, perceptions, and emotions of the investment committee members that dominate the discussion.

Further, the investment policy statement determines the design of the investment management structure. This structure reflects the attitudes and beliefs outlined in the investment policy statement, which asset classes (and sub-asset class segments) to invest in, the policy (or target) weighting for each, and their strategic ranges within the structure, views on active management versus a passive approach and, the performance standards (i.e., benchmarks, value-added targets, and time frames) assigned to effectively monitor the success of money managers and the fund structure over time.

As asset allocation dominates future fund risk and returns, even hiring the very best managers would not overcome a poorly designed investment policy.

Step 2: The Long List

Establishing the plan sponsor's manager selection process is basically no different to the steps taken when making short-term or long-term planning decisions within a typical business: 1) plan; 2) implement; and 3) control. In North America, for the vast majority of plan sponsors (outside of the mega funds, which may have the necessary internal staff resources and experience to manage their own fund assets), it is prudent to use consulting firms that specialize in assisting in the manager selection process. Working with a designated person within the organization or the selection sub-committee, the consultant can create a long list of candidates based on the plan sponsor's predetermined criteria.

Investment planning consultants typically have extensive databases on most money managers around the world to assist plan sponsors in choosing the most appropriate candidates for their specific mandates. However, it should be noted that investment consulting firms and individual consultants are not infallible or without biases. Some consulting organizations provide not only a manager selection service, but also an investment management platform (a package of external managers for use by clients). No matter how tight the internal controls, a conflict of interest could arise—the consultant could promote its own investment platform over what might be the better choice of outside managers.

As discussed in Chapter Four, consulting firms and individual consultants may have their manager favorites. The short list of candidates can differ significantly among consulting organizations. To make the scenario even more complex, manager choices may differ among investment consultants within the same organization. Moreover, different offices (e.g., London, New York, Tokyo, and Toronto) within the same firm may have different candidates based on a regional or country bias.

One major problem is that the investment committee members must have blind faith, as there is no way of telling whether an investment consulting firm is good at what it does, since there is no published track record confirming whether the manager selection process has been successful.

Consultants are agents of change. They tend to over-emphasize short-term performance and, at the same time, encourage manager search activity based on short-term disappointments. However, even with all the caveats, these consultants can provide significant assistance when entering a manager selection process. At the very least, you can point the finger their way if (or, quite likely, when) things go wrong. Refer to Chapter Four as a refresher on the biases and conflicts of interest within consulting organizations.

Consultant selection is clearly important, but it is beyond the scope of this book. However, there are a few of things to look for when hiring a consultant:

- the type and number of their clients;
- whether they have retainer-type clients or mostly undertake one-off projects;
- what their research depth is with regard to assessing both investment managers and alternative investments;
- whether they are proactive in the decision-making process;
- how they define risk;
- what the education and experience levels of their consultants are;
- whether there is diversity in their group;
- what the turnover of consultants within the organization has been and why;
- what education platforms they provide;
- how their consultants are remunerated;
- what reasons they provide for manager terminations;
- how extensive their manager database is;
- what their perceived conflicts of interest are; and,

- what weighting they place on manager ratings between qualitative and quantitative assessments.

Incidentally, if the consultant organization has a packaged manager platform, the investment committee members should ask how successful the platform has been (i.e., how many manager changes have been made and why?). Seeking this information could help to assess the consultant organization's skill at manager selection.

Step 3: The Lineup

In hiring a manager, the committee should consider several key areas to increase its chances of success.

Investment Management Organization

Investment management firms should have three basic policy statements:

1. a *vision* statement;
2. a *beliefs* statement; and,
3. a *values* statement.

Or, at the very least, they should have addressed all three issues in one form or another.

The vision statement outlines the "whats" of the organization. *What* are the longer-term goals and objectives? *What* are the necessary resources required to achieve these goals? *What* are the factors that will determine success? *What* events could trigger change in their basic business structure or direction? *What* factors give them an edge in delivering value-added returns and besting the competition? As an aside, I use "vision" rather than the commonly used term "philosophy"—which I believe gives managers way too much credit. It is not as if the investment management community is out combing the universe in search of the meaning of existence or knowledge within the investment field. However, they do (or should) have beliefs.

The beliefs statement focuses on the "whys" of the organization. *Why* has it chosen the path it is on (e.g., active vs. passive)? *Why* does it believe that its capital market segment will continue to provide it with opportunities to successfully exploit inefficiencies? *Why* has it chosen the investment style it has? *Why* does it believe that its decision-making structure and portfolio construction process will be able to create an effective balance between risk and return? *Why* does it believe it has assembled the best team of specialists to achieve the return objectives of its clients? Beliefs are the foundation for everything that follows.

A values statement highlights the "hows" of the organization. *How* can the firm provide a service that places its clients first? *How* can it foster an internal nurturing environment that ensures that all of its associates are treated fairly? *How* does it provide for a culture that is creative, diverse, and innovative with a continuous learning curve? *How* does it ensure an environment of accountability? *How* does it invest in or contribute to the community? Determining and assessing the culture of a money management organization is one of the most difficult tasks within the money management selection process.

When starting out on the quest to find the most desirable money manager, investment committee members must understand these statements to ensure that the managers' vision, beliefs, and values are consistent with the investment committee's own vision, beliefs, and values. If any one of these three areas do not align with the investment policy statement, then the manager might not be the right fit.

At this level, it is necessary to determine the *compensation structure* for the top professionals within the organization. Managers' compensation packages should be designed to align with the best interests of the client. Most compensation packages for portfolio managers have some link to the specific returns of their clients within the mandates that they manage. Some are team-driven performance bonuses, and some are based solely on the performance of individuals. However, in the majority of cases, I have found that bonuses related to client performance represent only a small segment of a manager's overall remuneration package (which may also include an organization's profit-sharing arrangement, dividends from share ownership, etc.). If performance achieves the value-added target or places above the median in a peer-group sample, the overall impact on the total yearly income package for the money manager might prove to be much less of an incentive than we are led to believe. Remuneration packages also differ by types of money management firms. Independent investment management firms likely have a greater emphasis on equity ownership than do financial institutions, which may focus more on team profit-sharing structures. There is no "perfect" remuneration structure. Money managers are motivated to move to the firms that pay the most.

Another important factor is *succession planning*. The investment committee members will want to know that, as investment professionals leave the organization for any reason, the vision, beliefs, and values of the organization will remain constant and consistent over time. The investment committee will also want to know who the next three main hires will be (in terms of positions, qualities, education, and experience) and what effect, if any, the loss of a key individual might have on their specific investment mandate.

Investment committee members should understand the following key issues when assessing investment management firms:

1. how the partners and owners within the firm define "success" (unfortunately, many firms define success as growth in assets under management—which is good for the firm but bad for the client);

2. how priorities have changed over time;

3. whether the investment decision-making process is driven by portfolio managers or research;

4. how the firm separates professional priorities from business priorities;

5. if the partners/owners had to start all over again, what they would do differently; and,

6. what the weaknesses are within the organization (there are always some weaknesses—if not, the partners/owners are not paying attention).

Firm Ownership

It is often stated that stock ownership within a money management firm is the glue that holds the team together—until it doesn't. Investment planning consultants ask members of the investment committee to highly value investment management organizations with broad equity distribution throughout the senior investment professionals. It is our intuitive nature to believe that ownership provides for longevity and continuity among investment professionals. In addition, most independent investment management firms have stock ownership as a main focus within their marketing presentations—all to provide comfort that, with skin in the game, all is well. This is not necessarily the case.

Share ownership might not be as much of a panacea to longevity and continuity as we are led to believe. However, the incentive, ownership, and succession structure is, nevertheless, critical to motivating and retaining the professional staff of the manager. The investment committee members would hope that the founding partners would be willing to develop a legacy for the firm by creating processes and procedures that ensure the firm can evolve efficiently and successfully from one generation to another. It is very rare that a money management firm being sold is in the best interest of the clients. The ideal situation is when a money management organization has a written succession plan.

People

Even in big, financial institutional firms, people are both the makers of the culture and the drivers of success. As a result, it is imperative to get to know the managers that an investment committee has selected, and those it is going to select, as best as possible. Performance is not the driving force in the selection process, while pay and ownership are also not the be-all and end-all; it is investment professionals who create the vision, beliefs, and values of a money management firm and are integral to the decision-making process. Whether for larger or smaller firms, culture is the driving force.

There is absolutely no substitute for visiting managers in their own habitat. The first step is to meet the members of the investment team who will be managing the portfolio. Even though the investment committee might be told that the team members are all equal in the decision-making process, there is typically one individual who stands out—the one who jumps in to answer your questions and who the other members seem to defer to. This is the main decision-maker. Once they have revealed themselves, most questions should now be directed to these individuals to determine whether they know what they are talking about.

The search might go sideways if the investment committee:

- has not clearly defined its objectives;
- misjudges the investment manager's experience and expertise;
- is ill-prepared for the interview process; or,
- has misaligned the goals and objectives with the selected manager.

The investment committee should also consider the following aspects:

1. A policy is required for how personal investment transactions are conducted. For example, are the investment specialists able to purchase individual securities that can also be purchased for their client's portfolio? Do they invest in their own funds (i.e., aligning their interest with those of their clients)? Do they need written approval from a compliance officer before a trade?

2. Smaller firms can be stretched a little thinner than larger firms. The investment committee should make sure that investment team members spend the vast majority of their time on portfolio management.

3. Investment committee members should be looking for good qualities in the individual and the team (e.g., chemistry, investment knowledge, seekers of new information and better insights, high ethical standards, alignment with client interests, and high energy levels). However, it is difficult to fully appreciate these "soft" attributes in just one or two meetings (e.g., how do you judge integrity up-front?). It serves no purpose to ask the money manager how it would rate its integrity level on a scale of 1 to 10. Investment committee members should ask for an example within the firm of when integrity became an issue and how it was resolved. There are always examples.

Investment committee members should look for an organization that has a competitive edge, a strong culture, unique or at least unusual insights, and a robust decision-making process that is executed with discipline and places clients first. The investment climate is always changing and what worked well yesterday might not work tomorrow. If there is a best-in-class manager out there, the fame and glory might carry the seeds of its own destruction. Good is probably as good as it gets, and, most likely, good enough. Also, examine their sell discipline.

Investment professionals tend to like what they do. They build their identity around their work. They choose their field because it appears to be exciting and challenging. At the early stages of their careers, they spend close to 100% of their time just on research and the construction of investment portfolios—typically, working longer than eight-hour days. However, as time marches on, investment specialists are pulled away from what they love best and what makes them happy. As the firm grows, other activities (i.e. marketing, servicing, and business management) start to eat up more and more time. As time progresses, portfolio managers can become alpha-challenged.

The takeaway here is how to conduct the interview process—the investment committee members should spend less time on reading the stated facts or claims, and more on reading the people.

Time Allocation

Within a money management firm, there are typically six time-consuming activities, as shown in Table 5.2 below:

TABLE 5.2: TYPICAL ACTIVITIES OF A MONEY MANAGER

	APPROXIMATE TIME ALLOCATION			
ACTIVITIES	**YEARS OF PROFESSIONAL EXPERIENCE**			
	0–5	**6–15**	**16–30**	**31–45**
Portfolio Management/Analysis	90%	75%	55%	50%
Marketing	—	5	10	15
Servicing	—	5	10	5
Administration	5	7	10	5
Business Management	—	—	5	10
Vacation Time	5	8	10	15
Total Time	100	100	100	100

A portfolio manager's career generally begins as a research analyst. Time spent on pure investment research in this role likely consumes more than 90% of the research analyst's time. It normally takes (or should take) 7 to 10 years for an analyst to evolve from an analyst function into portfolio management. As the portfolio manager begins to excel (assuming that they rank among the very best), these portfolio managers begin to spend more time in presentations to potential clients and their intermediaries (investment planning consultants), and servicing existing clients. As a result, more and more of the manager's time is spent in marketing and servicing roles. Here, their time is not only spent in presentations but also on preparation and travel.

As a rule of thumb, I believe that investment specialists should spend no less than 85% of their time on the investment management function. For servicing clients adequately, however, each money manager should be required to spend a minimum of five hours a quarter for each client—this includes time to get to and from meetings, as well as the presentation time in meetings. As a result, each client is allocated a minimum of 20 hours a year. With each working year having about 2,000 hours, and an allocation of, say, 10% of the total time for a portfolio manager in a servicing role, the portfolio manager would not be able to effectively service more than 10 to 12 clients—to maintain a minimum exposure of 85% on portfolio management. A manager's time for actual portfolio management can evaporate quickly. The investment committee should ask its money managers how many clients they have. As an aside, I believe the most important role for experienced marketing and servicing professionals is to protect the money managers from spending too much time on these functions.

Administration time increases when portfolio managers have a team reporting to them—having to spend time on hiring, training, motivating, evaluating, and retaining. In addition, with more experience, the portfolio manager begins to participate in internal business-oriented committees. After about 30 years of experience, the function of managing the firm's operations begins to take up more and more time—creating 5-year business plans, keeping up with technology advancements, addressing compliance issues, etc.

Vacation time also eats into the time of portfolio management—although I have not seen it addressed in any publications on investment management. Typically, in the early years, the investment analyst has two or three weeks of vacation. Between 10 and 15 years of experience, vacation time increases to more like four or five weeks. With over 25 years of experience, vacation time can expand to six to seven weeks—and I have come across some money managers who take three months off every year. Furthermore, the location of the manager's vacation property becomes a factor. If located two hours out of the city, the manager is likely to be leaving at noon on a Friday—and perhaps coming back to the office at noon on a Monday. If the vacation home requires a flight to get there and back, the time away from the office becomes still more of an issue. Even with technology these days, I do not believe that portfolio managers are as effective away from the office and the team as they are at the office. The important takeaway here is that time spent on portfolio management activities tends to ebb over time.

Performance

Just about anyone who has a view on the topic considers historical performance to be a poor (or considerably less than ideal) indicator of future performance—yet most money managers are selected based on their past performance results. Investment planning consultants slice and dice performance numbers within an inch of their lives. Consultants are big on attribution analysis—breaking down performance numbers by activity. Consultants don't believe that past results are useful, and they rarely assign any degree of statistical significance to them (although they could)—yet they can tell you to the penny exactly how the past results occurred. The numbers are very precise, just not prescient. This is like synchronizing your watches with a group of friends and stating that in *exactly* eight seconds, the time will be a *few* minutes after 3:00.

As for peer-group samples, the methodology on constructing the various samples (e.g., inclusion criteria) differ from one service provider to another. As a result, a money manager providing two measurement services with the same performance information could place in the second quartile in one sample and the third quartile in another sample—thus, it may be included in a search with one consulting firm and not with the other.

If you have a slight preference based on your qualitative assessments for a manager that places in the second quartile over one in the first quartile (consultants will not generally provide you with a short list of candidates that track below the median), do not be swayed by the numbers for the manager that places in the first quartile—the difference is, almost certainly, just noise. Return differences do not necessarily reflect quality differences.

The takeaway here is that the performance results the investment committee sees from the manager are soft, not totally reliable, and presented in the most favorable light possible. The committee should at least insist on all managers presenting results for the same set of periods, endpoints, and benchmarks.

Refer to Chapter Six, When Performance Measurement Goes Awry, for more detail on performance measurement analysis.

Step 4: Pick Me, Pick Me!

Based on the investment committee's judgment of the information gained in Step 3, it has culled its prospect list down to four to six finalists to present to the full investment committee. It is now time to set the agenda for the final presentations. By this time, the investment committee should have all the background information it will need going into this final round.

It is now time to set the stage for this final event—and when I say "set the stage," I mean it literally. In the current investment climate, plan sponsors are now dealing with well-honed "actors" who have been performing in final presentations for many years. Some investment management firms actually hire outside presentation specialists who train the investment professionals on how to win business. These image consultants work with the investment and marketing teams to craft their presentations. The investment professionals are put on camera and taught how to speak prospect-ese and project the right body language—right down to the type and color of suit to wear, removing any references to sports analogies, not drinking cold water before the presentation as this might constrict the vocal cords, etc. The presentation package has been clinically prepared to "wow." So, the final presentation is mostly an "act"—just so you know.

The Traditional Approach

Usually, with the assistance of a consultant, an agenda is put together to cover the four Ps: 1) philosophy; 2) people; 3) process; and 4) performance (five Ps if "fees" were spelled "phees"). For a two-hour meeting, the agenda would look something like Figure 5.1 below:

FIGURE 5.1: HYPOTHETICAL AGENDA OF A TWO-HOUR MEETING

AGENDA	
Philosophy: *(30 minutes)* - Organization - History - Beliefs	**Process:** *(60 minutes)* - Research/construction - Selection (buys and sells) - Controls (risks)
People: *(20 minutes)* - Education - Experience - Roles	**Performance:** *(10 minutes)* - Benchmark/value-added - Peer comparisons - Attribution

Experienced, successful investment specialists have seen this style of agenda many, many times. There is likely not a question that comes up that they have not heard before—and are not prepared to address. However, pretty much all the information that is expected in the final presentation is, or should have been, available from the money managers long before the actual presentation. The main reason for having a final presentation from the money managers is that most investment committee members do not spend the time reading and understanding the pertinent information before these meetings. In a well-designed selection process, all finalists should be able to effectively manage the investment committee's mandate—if not, what are they doing in the finals? In reality, the final pick is typically the firm that is the most elegant in its presentation—the reason it is often referred to as a "beauty contest."

Also, the agenda is typically sent out to the managers in advance so they have time to practice—setting up a dry rehearsal run on their part. The stage is set to their advantage—not for the investment committee's.

AND NOW FOR SOMETHING COMPLETELY DIFFERENT:

The first thing the investment committee should do is set the ground rules for the final presentations. This is the committee's show—not the managers' show. The investment committee should insist that its members read the summarized material prepared by the selection committee ahead of time—even meeting with committee members and the investment planning consultant ahead of the meeting with the manager candidates so that committee members know what to look for and what to expect. The committee should not send out an agenda to the money managers ahead of time. If the managers really know their stuff, one will not be necessary. The actual agenda should be set in your format, in your order, and given the time allocation for each topic based on the information you require to make the decision on which manager to hire. Investment committee members should ask questions whenever they want—not to be disruptive, but to gain clarification and understanding on the topic being discussed.

The committee can tell the money managers that they can bring their presentation packages with them (they apparently need these as a security blanket). However, the packages will be handed out only at the end of the meeting, and relevant pages will be shown during the meeting only if essential to clarify a point in answering a question. I know that this format puts some pressure on the investment committee to follow along, but the members get to see how the managers cope without their visual aids.

Also, it is very difficult for investment committee members to listen to a speaker, watch the slide presentation, and read through the presentation package all at the same time. One of these three will dominate—and it is likely to differ for each committee member. Also, committee members are sometimes impatient and flip ahead. This is disruptive to both the presenter and other committee members. When a committee member's head is buried in a presentation, it is virtually impossible to read a money manager's body language. It is useful for committee members to take notes throughout the session to compare with other members at the end of the presentation—even better if these presentation meetings are recorded.

As a concession, the managers could be allowed to bring no more than five slides with them to hand out or show during the meeting. This will give the investment committee members a good idea of what the manager feels is important enough to emphasize to the committee. Hopefully, the manager will not waste time showing performance data on one of the pages, as they have already cleared that hurdle. In fact, in the final presentation, performance should not be addressed at all—it has already been analyzed and presenting it again is a waste of precious time.

One unique feature about investment management firms is how similar they all look, given their specific investment styles. Managers may refer to their decision-making process as being "unique" or having a "competitive edge"—or that they have pertinent information that no one else has. These statements assume that the firm you are looking at knows the decision-making processes of all the other investment management firms out there. They don't. No firms are unique in the way the investment committee would hope. Furthermore, in relatively efficient markets, almost all information is known—what differs are the interpretations that various managers place on the information.

The question is how to differentiate one money manager from another. Most managers have way too many "motherhood" statements: (e.g., "we look at world-class companies only," "we operate with a high degree of integrity," and "we put our clients first"). An investment committee wants answers to its members' questions that can be proved, confirmed, or verified. These motherhood statements do not help in any way.

Once again, the investment committee members should remember that this is *their* meeting, under their rules. To keep the meetings progressing on time (usually allowing two to three hours per manager to remain within limits), bring along a timer that is visible to the presenters to let them know that you are serious about keeping the meeting moving along. Managers tend to answer questions that have not been asked, ignore questions that have been asked, and repeat themselves after about five minutes of uninterrupted talking. I have never heard an answer to any question that needed more than two minutes for a full explanation—and finishing within one minute is even better.

Visions, Beliefs, and Values

The investment committee should know what vision the partners/owners have for the firm going forward. How will the firm look 5 or 10 years down the road—and why? What resources will be required to meet its goals and objectives? What products will be introduced—and why? For existing products, will there be any closings (hard or soft)? Why is one style chosen over another? What changes have occurred since inception—and why? No changes might mean the firm is not learning or keeping up with trends in the outside world—which might affect its competitive edge or conviction. Too many changes could reflect that things aren't working out as well as it had hoped, or that it has lost its focus. The important thing is how much money is being reinvested back into the firm, and where.

Investment Professionals

The investment committee should know the time allocation of the investment team members. To find this out, the committee should provide a form, such as that shown in Table 5.2 above for the managers to fill out during the meeting with regard to their own time.

The committee should aim to know the diversity within the team: education, years of experience (both with the firm and with other firms), age, gender, etc. If members of the mandate team or other senior professionals have left the organization, committee members should know why—and where they went (if members retired or moved into a different career, there might not be a problem; if professionals have departed to join other investment management firms, this could be the result of a poor culture).

The investment committee should know how the team members make decisions. In this regard, I have noted two points over my 50-plus years in the investment management business, including as an investment planning consultant: first, a team of more than four members may result in too much compromising. The bets become smaller and the portfolios become more conservative with each new member added to the team. A team with two members might not have the diversity (i.e., might be too like-minded) and lack balance to be objective. Second, as discussed earlier when regarding investment committee membership, it is not necessarily the smartest person in the room, the one with the most experience, or the one with the best ideas who gets heard. It is generally the team member who pounds the desk the hardest and longest. It is important to find the real decision-maker. I have found that the most effective teams have three to four members—if diverse.

Within the team structure, the investment committee should know whether the manager operates off an "approved list" or uses a "model portfolio"—and how much discretion each manager has when constructing their portfolios. In addition, is there accountability in covering each individual security and sector in the portfolio for ongoing monitoring control? If so, is there one member on the team who has more coverage than others? Finally, the committee should know how many client accounts the team is managing and how much of the total assets under management is represented by the largest two or three clients. This information will hopefully give committee members an idea of the team members' capacity to manage their investment portfolios.

Controls

The investment committee needs to know what internal controls are in place to ensure that managers act with a high degree of integrity, and in the fund's best interest. One point relates to how investment professionals are monitored. Where are the compliance people located? They should be placed outside of the investment division and should be independent in their role of overseeing the total investment operation—from the top layer of the CEO and president down. It is important that the investment committee members understand the compliance process—to ensure there is accountability.

A few final points:

- What, if any, affiliations do the money managers have and, if there are any, will they result in a conflict of interest?
- What is the full range of products and services available?
- How is diversification achieved (i.e., risk-control measures)?
- What are the largest and smallest client sizes in the mandate the investment committee has chosen for the fund?
- What is the portfolio turnover and how has it changed over time?
- Has the investment management organization or its professionals ever been involved in any litigation, claims, assessments, or regulatory investigations?
- What are its servicing capabilities and communication methods?
- Finally, what is the investment manager's golf handicap (the higher, the better—perhaps a sign of less time spent away from the office)?

During the final presentation, it is fairly easy to identify the "alpha." Then, all further questions should be directed to the *other* investment professional(s). One of three things will happen:

1. the alpha lets the other person talk with no interruptions or add-ons at the end (this is rare, but, if it materializes, is a fairly good sign that the firm culture is inclusive and respectful);
2. the alpha interrupts or makes additions for clarity (this is perhaps not a totally cohesive team effort); or,
3. the alpha corrects others' responses (this perhaps indicates poor teamwork).

Portfolio Characteristics

Portfolios may change over time for reasons other than pure investment decisions, including an increase in assets under management, which might negatively affect the value-added target above the benchmark (not meeting performance expectations), a change in team membership, a change in the focus of the firm, a change in the investment style, and the time allocation of the professionals. The investment committee should aim to see if it can follow the characteristics of the portfolio over time (e.g., snapshots at intervals over the last three to five years, and any major transactions).

For example, to assess whether portfolio size and growth have had any impact on the portfolio, the investment committee members should know the number of securities held in the mandate, the sector deviation measurement (variance in the sector weightings in the portfolio vs. those in the benchmark), and the average capitalization size against the benchmark—10 years ago, 5 years ago, and now. For investment style, the investment committee should know how the mandate's value or growth characteristics have changed over time, as well as the portfolio turnover of the investment mandate—10 years ago, 5 years ago, and now.

This information would show the committee members whether the portfolio characteristics in the desired mandate are drifting and becoming more benchmark-like. If so, the historical value-added performance reported will likely not be repeated in the future. If expectations are lower, the investment committee has to determine whether lower is good enough.

Performance

"The truth, the whole truth, and nothing but the truth" are words seldom spoken by the presenters of performance data.

All performance results should be calculated by a third party. They should be transparent and guaranteed by the independent provider with regard to construction procedures and methodology. The investment committee should be aware of the following issues:

- For composites, what percentage of the accounts in the mandate is excluded, and why?

- What is the dispersion of the performance from clients' performance and that of the composite?

- Are the numbers certified and do they meet the performance standards outlined by CFA Institute?

Performance numbers are very period-sensitive and end-point dependent. Moving out just one quarter in looking at four-year, moving-average time horizons could change a manager's placement in a peer-group sample from the third to the second quartile, or vice versa.

Money Management Fees

Sliding fee schedules are the norm within the investment management industry, and are fairly consistent across all managers with similar mandates (both domestic and global for traditional equity and fixed-income assignments, with greater variance among non-traditional asset class segments). Money managers must stay somewhat competitive with fees if they cannot distinguish their mandate through performance. If the fund has significant assets, it may be possible to negotiate fees, resulting in just one or two fee breakpoints. If the fund doesn't have a size advantage, it is more difficult to negotiate fees—although it is not impossible.

As indicated in Chapter Four, for some mandates, clients may have "most-favored nation" clauses—an arrangement in which fees are equalized to the lower level for clients with the same asset size and similar objectives. However, as stated earlier, this is difficult to prove, as managers can always find a way to show how any one client is different enough from another.

Nevertheless, for the plan sponsor's mandate, committee members should ask whether there are any clients with incentive-based fee structures or most-favored nation clauses, how long the fees are guaranteed for, how fees are calculated, and the manager's billing procedures.

Step 5: Aligned Interests

When entering an investment manager search, and at the stage of interviewing manager candidates, committee members should be aware of one major, potential conflict of interest inherent in many money management organizations: ensuring that each management organization places the interests of its clients over that of the organization and the professionals who will be managing your portfolio. The client must always come first.

Plan sponsors should never assume that just because it is the right thing to do, it will be done. The problem these days is that money management organizations can be managing monies for different client types with different financial goals.

Serving More Than One Master

There are basically four types of distribution channels that can be housed within a money management firm:

1. institutional-type funds (e.g., pension and institutional accounts, operating and endowment funds, foundations, charitable organizations, and insurance assets);

2. mutual funds;

3. private wealth individuals or families; and,

4. third-party platforms.

The fee structure and profit margins are different for each of these channels—with mutual funds having the highest fee schedule, and pension and other institutional-type funds having the lowest. Each of these distribution channels is likely to have different goals and objectives. In some firms, there may be separate asset class teams that serve each of the client types—in other firms (perhaps smaller firms), the same investment team may be managing portfolios that attempt to create investment funds that fit two or more of these client types. With more than one distribution channel, it is important for the investment committee members to find out where its fund ranks in the pecking order—where are the manager's business priorities, and how are they monitored? Investment committee members should just be aware and ask the manager about its security allocation process and procedures for how priorities are set and monitored.

As a general theme throughout this book, I am strongly opposed to any activity of the money manager or the consultant that results in one client having a preferential advantage over another client.

Step 6: After the Ball

A final step is required to complete the money manager selection process. The new manager needs to thoroughly understand the plan sponsor's return expectations, tolerance and appetite for risk, measurement criteria, timeframe, and any specific guidelines or constraints. The focus should be on exceptional communication skills to bridge the typically high language barrier and knowledge disparity between plan sponsors and investment managers. What one party says, the other might not hear or interpret correctly. At this early stage of the partnership, it is in the interests of both parties to begin the journey with a thorough understanding of what the plan sponsor expects, and what the investment manager can deliver. Without time and effort put in at this stage, the partnership has a low chance of survival.

Servicing

Typically, when selecting a money manager, there tends to be very little (if any) focus on how the relationship will work going forward. However, the relationship manager is likely to be the closest relationship that the plan sponsor has with the manager—it is perhaps the most important relationship.

Before signing on the dotted line, the investment committee members should ask the following questions of the management firm:

- What is the firm's servicing model? Is the servicing role within the firm designed as a career path, or used as a stepping-stone to some other area within the firm? How is the servicing structure integrated into the other areas of the organization?

- How is the relationship manager compensated? What are the measurements for success?

- How much authority does the relationship manager have?

- How are relationship managers chosen? What qualities are considered? Do relationship managers attend the investment strategy meetings?

- How is client coverage determined?

- How many client relationships does the relationship manager have, and for what mandates?

- How has client servicing changed within the firm over the past five years?

It is important for the plan sponsor to outline its servicing requirements. Once again, before signing the contract, the plan sponsor should meet with the person who will be covering the account. Check their experience level, background, education, servicing load (their smallest and largest clients), and capability. It is important to ensure the right fit.

TERMINATING A MANAGER

The good news is that firing a manager is far easier than hiring one. The following are examples of just a few valid reasons that could result in a manager's termination:

- *Turnover:* A red flag would be raised if any of the investment professionals hired by the plan sponsor, and who were an integral part of the decision-making process, were to leave. If not satisfied with the remaining/replacement team, the plan sponsor should terminate the money manager relationship. If clients are exiting the mandate the plan sponsor has selected, this might also be a concern. Another source of concern is if portfolio activity is excessive without the desired results.

- *Ownership change*: The main attributes of investment professionals are their passion for the job, commitment to the process, and loyalty to the firm (and, hopefully, to their clients). If the incentives change, these attributes might disappear. I have yet to see a money management firm that has been sold to another money management firm that was in the best interest of the clients.

- *Size*: A firm that is growing so fast that its personnel and infrastructure are not able to keep pace could result in the portfolio manager overseeing too many accounts—with less time for managing the assets. Furthermore, asset growth within the selected mandate may result in smaller and smaller portfolio bets and, therefore, a lower ability to deliver alpha.

- *Loss of their competitive advantage*: This occurs where outside influences have reduced or eliminated the edge the manager might have had.

- *Mandate breach*: This occurs when there is a material failure to comply with the written mandate without sufficient justification and remedy.

- *Poor servicing*: Not being kept up-to-date on happenings within the firm might prove to be detrimental to continuing the relationship—resulting in lack of credibility and confidence, or lack of access to the portfolio manager. Servicing is the only activity that money management organizations have control over.

- *More attractive alternatives*: Termination might be suitable when there is a money manager or investment management organization with the same potential and attributes as an existing manager—however, at a significantly lower cost.

- *Change in fund characteristics*: The plan sponsor might consider termination if the goals and objectives at the plan level have changed—resulting in a review of the money management structure and/or the managers.

- *Beliefs*: As markets change and passive approaches become more attractive than active strategies (or vice versa), it might be suitable to seek another manager.

- *Lost trust/lost confidence*: Concerns that the manager has lost the skill and experience needed to deliver the desired results might merit termination.

- *Performance*: I have deliberately placed "performance" as the last reason to consider when firing a manager. Recent studies have shown that the performance of terminated managers is likely to be higher in the two years after termination than that of the managers being hired (i.e., the probabilities of a fourth-quartile manager being above the median within two years of termination is higher than the first-quartile manager being above the median). We tend to place too much emphasis on short-term performance—which may result in higher money manager turnover than is necessary. Again, short-term performance is basically just noise.

Terminating a manager carries a significant cost, including both market-impact costs and commissions associated with portfolio turnover. The typical transition cost is estimated to be in the range of 1% to 2% of the assets transferred—depending on the specific mandate. Furthermore, there is the cost of the change agent who assisted in providing a list of potential candidates, and the cost of human capital of the committee members required to establish a short list of candidates, meet in their offices, listen to final presentations, etc.

All too often, firing a manager is an emotional decision that is taken for the wrong reasons and at the wrong time.

Some final observations:

- All succession plans of the money managers should be provided in writing.

- Money manager compensation packages should be tied as closely as possible to the longer-term and shorter-term goals and objectives of the clients. Plan sponsors should know what percentage of the portfolio manager's package is fixed versus variable, what percentage of the variable component is short term versus longer term, and how this is determined.

- Plan sponsors should know what percentage of the money management organization's profits are being reinvested back into the organization—and where, why, and how this has changed over the past five years. Knowing this information may assist in understanding the outlined succession plan. If a good percentage of the profits is being reinvested in the firm, it might indicate that the firm is building for generations to come. If the vast majority of the profits walk out the door with the partners/owners every night—perhaps the firm is being groomed to be sold.

- It is important to know how investment professionals are hired—what are the criteria and attributes that the money management organization is looking for?

- The manager selection process is basically a process of elimination. It is human nature to focus on the negatives, and so, the plan sponsor starts to look for flaws within the money manager candidates—reasons to cull them from the herd. Generally, it is the last organization standing that wins the assignment. If the screening of potential candidates is effective, one manager should not really stand out from the others.

- Money manager selection is important, but not as important as one might think—as the asset mix decision is the main driving force for total fund returns and risk tolerance.

- Finally, investment management firms are a business, typically run by investment management professionals. The focus is on profits and, as a result, the products and the clients with the highest margins likely receive the most attention.

In summary, the manager selection process is one of the primary responsibilities of the investment committee—it is also one of the most difficult and time consuming. Three factors that seem to be consistently important when selecting managers are:

1. having a well-defined ownership structure or profit-sharing plan that is fair and equitable among investment professionals—along with an excellent succession plan;

2. low turnover of investment professionals and others throughout the organization—as well as low client turnover; and,

3. control over the growth of assets under management that allows for continued value-added results—where execution is not a negative factor.

There is no foolproof way to ensure success in the manager search process. The goal of the investment committee is not to pick a future winner; rather it is to reduce the chance of failure—as failure is very costly. If one manager is exchanged for another, the plan sponsor will move from a manager whose style and approach has not been rewarded in the marketplace to one whose style and approach has been rewarded—but might not continue to be in a different future environment.

So, for performance measurement, here are the facts:

1. benchmarks for comparing a money manager's performance may prove to be inappropriate and sending the wrong message if they are not representative of the specific mandate;

2. peer-group samples have flaws owing to inclusion criteria, biases, and time sensitivity; and,

3. overall, performance results are a poor indicator of future performance results.

This reality does not provide a lot of confidence for investment committee members. The investment committee members are creating investment policy and making decisions in an uncertain, imperfect, and ever-changing investment environment. Committee members do not have the luxury of resting.

The first decision investment committee members should make is on their belief whether the various components of the capital market are efficient or not. If the members believe that active management can exploit market inefficiencies and anomalies, producing value-added returns over and above the benchmark and the cost of active management, then active is the way to go. As indicated throughout this chapter, the process of selecting and retaining a money management organization is time consuming—if done correctly. Outside of the decision related to formulating an appropriate asset mix policy, the next most important function of the committee is to select a manager that will enhance returns at the total fund level.

Bottom line: The choice for the investment committee members comes down to whether above-benchmark results can be achieved over time and above the inherent costs of active management, and whether committee members believe they have the skill and experience to find and select these managers.

CHAPTER SIX

WHEN PERFORMANCE MEASUREMENT GOES AWRY

Things Are Not Always What They Seem

Just a thought:

A recent survey found that 93.126% of
the population will believe any statistic
if it is taken out three decimal places.

INTRODUCTION

One of the major contributions to business management from the 1950s was the concept of "management by objectives" (MBO). This concept was first introduced in 1954 by Peter Drucker in his seminal book, *The Practice of Management*. MBO was incubated in the 1960s and took hold in the 1970s. As proposed by Drucker, objectives were to be established to accomplish five ideals:

1. to organize and explain the entire range of business phenomena in a small number of general statements;
2. to test these statements in actual experience;
3. to predict behavior;
4. to appraise the soundness of decisions while they were still being made; and,

5. to enable practicing businesses to analyze their own experience and, as a result, improve performance.

Given the size of the North American pension fund market (well over U.S. $17 trillion, as estimated by the OECD), it may be assumed that, with all the information at one's fingertips, the massive amount of portfolio management tools, and the ultrasophisticated performance measurement techniques that have evolved over the past six decades, we would have an excellent handle on measuring the ongoing success or failure of the investment fund itself (the primary decisions made at the plan sponsor level) and the capital market components (the strategy implementation by the money managers). In my experience, this has not been the case. I believe that this inability to measure success or failure effectively has cost the pension industry hundreds of millions of dollars over the past decade through the firing of managers at the wrong time and for the wrong reasons—as well as the hiring of managers at the wrong time and for the wrong reasons.

Performance standards are determined by the investment committee members at the total fund level and for each of the mandates included within the investment management structure. These standards include a representative *benchmark*, a reasonable *value-added target*, and a *timeframe* for measurement purposes to determine success.

BENCHMARKING DEFINED

Benchmarking has emerged as the primary tool for measuring success or failure within the investment management community. The term is widely used, but can mean very different things to different players in the investment field, including plan sponsors, consultants, and money managers.

CFA Institute has defined what a benchmark is for the investment management community. CFA Institute states that: "Benchmarks are important tools to aid in the planning, implementation and review of investment policy. They clarify communication between the investment fiduciary and the investment manager and provide a point of departure for assessing return and risk." A benchmark is "essentially the starting point for evaluating success." Its specific benchmark definition is as follows: "An independent rate of return (or hurdle rate) forming an objective test of the effective implementation of an investment strategy."

CFA Institute determines what makes a good benchmark as follows: "A benchmark should be a focal point in the relationship between the manager and the fiduciary body overseeing the prudent management of the assets. The thoughtful choice of a benchmark will make the relationship between these parties more effective and enhance the value of the investment strategy." As stated in Chapter Three, the most effective benchmarks are specified in advance, relevant, measurable, unambiguous, representative of current investment opinions, accountable, investable, and complete.

CFA Institute further states that "choosing a bad or inappropriate benchmark can undermine the effectiveness of an investment strategy and lead to dissatisfaction between client and manager."

The overall objective of performance measurement is to assess ongoing performance by providing measurable standards for the plan sponsor to ensure that it achieves its longer-term goals.

Bottom line: If the benchmark is inappropriate, then any analytics compared to the benchmark would be suspect. The main objective is to create a benchmark that adequately reflects the money manager's investment style, decision-making process, and portfolio construction criteria. Overall, the benchmark should reflect the manager's universe for security selection and investment strategy.

THE THREE PRIMARY BENCHMARKS

As highlighted in Chapter Two, over the years, there have been three main bogeys available in the performance measurement of pension and investment funds: *absolute*, *comparative*, and *relative*.

Absolute: Target-Based

The primary measurement yardstick in the 1950s and 1960s was inflation—generally, the consumer price index (CPI) measured against the fund as a whole. During these two decades, inflation in North America averaged about 2.5% per annum. The thinking was that if the fund return exceeded the inflation rate, assets would outpace liabilities and create a surplus that could reduce the cost of funding the plan by the plan sponsor and/or enable it to increase benefits. It was assumed that the overall return from the components of the capital market would exceed inflation by some margin. As a result, money managers were typically given a value-added target above the rate of inflation, generally 3% to 4%. For example, if inflation over a 10-year moving-average time period was 3%, then the money manager would be expected to deliver a return of 6% to 7% on the assets managed. As the benchmark was inflation based, the measurement period generally was over a longer-term time horizon of 5 to 10 years. Given the embryonic state of the pension and investment industry back then, an inflation-based target was not that unreasonable a benchmark. Indexes were still in their infancy.

This benchmark worked well (given no alternatives) until the hyper-inflationary environment of the late 1970s and early 1980s, when it became virtually impossible to outperform the inflation-driven benchmark.

Comparative: Peer-Group Sampling

In the early 1960s, peer-group comparisons started to become popular. The idea was that by placing stock managers, bond managers, and balanced fund managers within carefully constructed peer groups, the pension and investment communities would be able to compare and determine the good managers from the bad. The performance of the various money managers would be placed into quartiles. Managers could then be evaluated in both up markets and down markets. Being basically the only measurement game in town, the peer-group sampling concept thrived, and money managers began to be hired and fired based on comparative performance within their peer group. As there was now a way to distinguish one manager from another based on performance, manager search activity began to increase, resulting in new service providers entering into the market (e.g., actuarial firms, investment planning consulting firms, independent, money management firms, and performance measurement firms).

In the 1970s and 1980s, peer-group sampling had become the primary measurement tool for plan sponsors and other investors to measure investment success at both the total fund level and the money managers within the investment management structure—with inflation comparisons becoming a far distant second.

Relative 1: Index Driven

A third measurement source began to emerge around the mid-1980s—measuring performance relative to market indexes. At that time, passive/index managers became an alternative option to active management. If active managers could not outperform the designated index selected as the benchmark (even before fees), then why have active management at all—given the much higher fees and the perceived risk of going active?

Passive/index providers began to flourish by creating more and more ways to slice the components of the capital market. In the mid-1980s to mid-1990s, macro indexes began to be segmented (e.g., large-cap, mid-cap, and small-cap equities; short-term, mid-term, and long-term bonds; government, corporate, and high-yield bonds, etc.). In the mid-1990s, investment-style indexes emerged—and the nine-box matrix was formed, with value, growth, and blend/market-oriented investment styles on one scale, and large-, mid-, and small-cap capitalization segments on the other.

As passive/index approaches provided an alternative to active managers, a value-added target for active managers was added to the predetermined index/passive-oriented benchmarks selected. For example, the investment management agreement of the plan sponsor might use the S&P 500 Index as the benchmark with a value-added target of, say, 100 basis points above the benchmark over four-year, moving-average timeframes. This value-added target would hopefully exceed the fees of active management.

As a result, from the 1990s on, index-driven hurdle rates became the primary investment performance benchmark, with peer-group comparisons relegated to second place. Two things occurred at this time: first, the emphasis shifted from measuring the fund as a whole to measuring, in detail, the component parts of the fund managed by the money managers. Second, attribution of value-added results could now be tracked. Under peer-group sampling, as the characteristics of the median within a peer-group sample were not known, performance attribution against the median could not be calculated.

Relative 2: Custom Designed/Goal Based

Benchmarking has become significantly more sophisticated in the past two decades—and significantly more complicated. With the tools available to analyze performance results in greater detail, plan sponsors and investment planning consultants are in a better position to determine manager "skill"—not that they necessarily can, just that they are in a better position to be able to do so.

Now, at this stage, index providers have moved from creating cap-based indexes and investment-style indexes to trying to understand the manager's exact universe for security selection and the specified investment process and approach for selecting from their universe. As a result, index providers and consultants have begun to create custom-designed benchmarks to better determine and isolate a manager's skill. Money managers can now be measured against an investment-style index as well as within an investment-style peer-group sample. In addition to attempting to determine a manager's skill, these custom-designed benchmarks assist in creating appropriate value-added targets if a plan sponsor wishes to implement an incentive-based fee structure.

In summary, there has been a significant shift in how investment performance is measured. Under the inflation-based period of the 1950s and 1960s, managers were expected to do the best they could. There really were no diversification rules or risk metrics. Through the 1970s and 1980s comparison within a peer-group sample was now the primary measurement tool for determining a money manager's success. Although peer-group sampling had its weaknesses, it was basically the only game in town in these two decades. In the 1990s, benchmarking against a predetermined index/passive bogey ushered in an alternative to active management. Although passive management had been around since the 1970s, it wasn't until the various overseers of investment management established performance standards against market indexes that passive/index approaches became a viable alternative to active management.

As an aside, even though the primary benchmark is passive/index driven, most investment management searches take place because the money manager places below the median within its investment-style peer group.

BENCHMARK USES

Within the pension and investment communities, there are six main uses where benchmarking becomes a factor:

- *Total fund*: Indexes are used as proxies for the various asset classes at the total fund level to formulate asset mix policy. Historical returns, volatility of those returns, and the correlation of returns from one asset class to another are used to assist investment committees and consultants in determining an appropriate asset class mix, the policy/target weight, and specified upper/lower tolerances ranges for each asset class. At the total fund level, a blended benchmark can, generally, be created to match the target weights of each of the asset classes used within the investment management structure. This allows investment committee members to assess whether the decisions *they* are making actually add value to total fund performance.

- *Money manager performance*: As stated in Chapter One, the money manager has a relatively small role to play within the investment management structure in generating significant, additional value-added performance beyond the asset mix decision. However, the money managers get the most attention. As indicated in the introduction in this chapter, the performance returns of the money managers are sliced and diced in detail against the selected benchmarks. With an appropriate benchmark, this is the most effective way to assess money management performance and to determine skill.

- *Passive alternatives*: In some asset class segments, it might be difficult to create value-added results after both the risks and costs of active management are factored in. For example, many studies (by academics and passive/index providers) have shown how difficult it is for active, large-cap equity managers to outperform the S&P 500 over the longer term—with the U.S. equity market being the most efficient market in the world. As a result, passive strategies have become either as the core holding within a specific asset class with active specialty management as a complement, or as a pure substitute for active strategies.

- *Money management compensation*: Most money managers attempt to align their interests with their clients. As a result, if money managers achieve the performance targets set out by their clients, they might be eligible for performance bonuses.

- *Incentive-based fees*: Incentive-based fees can be initiated by either the plan sponsor, the money manager, or the consultant. These fees are typically triggered after a money manager has exceeded a specified value-added target over the benchmark.

- *Attribution analysis*: It is important for plan sponsors to know how performance results were generated (e.g., from market timing, sector weightings, security selection, and timing) to help answer the question whether managers have delivered the returns due to skill or luck.

Refer to Chapter Eight, Incentive-Based Fees, for a more detailed discussion on incentive-based fees.

SO, WHAT COULD GO WRONG?

There is one truism in the investment industry: past performance is not a predictor of future performance. So, with all the sophisticated tools now at the disposal of the investment committee members, we are only marginally ahead of determining manager "skill"—and whether this will translate into above-average performance (against any bogey selected or against expectations) in the future—than we were two or three decades ago. We have become a lot better at determining the reasons for how managers earned that extra cent—we just have very little idea how to generate that extra cent in the future. The whole process is a little like driving while looking in the rear-view mirror.

What makes measuring money manager performance difficult over time is that there are so many moving parts. This section highlights some of the problems with focusing too closely on the three measurement tools discussed earlier in this chapter.

Inflation-Driven

This bogey does not meet any of the criteria outlined by CFA Institute in terms of what constitutes an "effective" benchmark. It is not *representative* of an asset class, not *transparent*, not *investable*, and not *representative* of a manager's style or approach. Furthermore, inflation (as measured by the CPI) can be revised over time and the basket of goods incorporated within the CPI might not reflect the true inflation rate within the economy—as consumer tastes and habits change more rapidly than do changes in the CPI basket. As a result, inflation-driven benchmarks are now very rare—and only used at the total fund level.

Peer-Group Sampling

As mentioned earlier in this chapter, peer-group sampling now plays a backup role to passive/index-focused benchmarks. However, investment managers are still typically hired or fired based on comparative performance. A manager that achieves its performance against its bogey (the index plus the hoped-for value-added target) could be terminated if the portfolio placed in the third or fourth quartile of a peer-group sample—the manager would have achieved the primary goal, but fallen short on the secondary objective (i.e., over 50% of managers were able to achieve a higher value-added return). Alternatively, the manager could have fallen short on the primary objective, but placed in the second quartile and keeps the client (i.e., over 50% of the managers found it difficult to add significant value against the benchmark). Thus, peer-group sampling as a measurement tool creates the most manager turnover activity—the manager should have done better against its competition. If money managers underperformed the benchmark, they can point out that so too did 60% of their closest peers, and therefore, delivered second quartile comparative performance. In other words, the message is: if you think my performance is bad, you should see how the other money managers did. It is the old tattletale and point-the-finger approach to deflect attention.

As with the inflation bogey, peer-group sampling does not meet the criteria of an effective measuring stick—it is not *representative* of any asset class or mandate, not *specified* in advance, not *transparent*, and not *investable*. In fact, the median fund does not exist.

As well, there are a number of biases associated with peer-group sampling:

- *Composition bias*: Measurement service providers gather information from various sources that can (and do) result in different quartile breaks for various asset classes and asset class segments for each measurement service—even though the heading for each grouping might appear to be the same from one service provider to another. A manager providing the same information on the same portfolio to two different service providers could find itself placing in the second quartile in one sample and third quartile in the other.

- *Construction bias*: Measurement service providers have different criteria for the construction of their various samples (e.g., an equal-weighted sample vs. a portfolio-weighted sample, commingled funds vs. segregated portfolios, specialty portfolios vs. components of a balanced fund, and money manager portfolios vs. plan sponsor funds). When using a performance measurement service, the investment management committee members should understand the construction methodology.

- *Selection bias*: Money managers generally have control over the timing of when they want to include a portfolio or fund within a sample. It is unlikely that a manager will choose to include a portfolio that is not doing well—if it is up to the manager.

- *Misclassification bias*: Measurement services attempt to place money managers with "like" managers. However, this becomes difficult when a manager has exposure to more than one characteristic or factor. A manager could find itself placed in different boxes by the various measurement services. In addition, investment-style drift could arise as markets force managers to adjust their investment style.

- *Size bias*: The size of the sample becomes important. As manager investment styles have become more defined, more samples have emerged, resulting in the sample sizes becoming smaller. Outliers can skew these samples. To combat this bias, some measurement services have removed the portfolios/funds that place within the top 5% and bottom 5% of the sample.

- *Inclusion bias*: Measurement services attempt to be the first out of the gate at the end of each quarter with their samples—a branding issue, as the first on the scene gets quoted in financial publications. As a result, money management firms that did not submit their information on time might be excluded from a sample that they were in the previous quarter—creating a sampling error. In addition, some portfolios/funds in the sample may place specific investment constraints on the portfolio/fund that could be detrimental to overall performance during certain time periods.

- *Survivorship bias*: This occurs when portfolios (typically, poorly performing funds) are removed from a sample. If the history is removed, only the better-performing portfolios/funds remain—resulting in the historical median return moving up.

Another caveat is never knowing who the top performing managers are, what styles are working, whether there are client constraints, and what the risk level is.

I believe there are enough concerns with peer-group sampling for it not to be the primary reason for hiring or firing managers. Yes, I know that investment committees do not typically hire managers that are currently in the third or fourth quartile of a sample (even though doing so may be the best option for the performance of the investment fund); however, I also believe that investment committees are too quick to fire their managers who fall into the third or even fourth quartile, without an in-depth analysis of why performance appears to be below expectations.

Index Comparisons

Comparing performance results against a passive-driven index meets virtually all the criteria of an effective benchmark—that part is good. However, even indexes have flaws. There can be a difference between indexes that are constructed by a committee within the index service provider or by some predetermined formula. An index could be market-cap weighted versus market-float weighted, or equal-cap weighted. And then there is the timing for rebalancing the securities within the index as circumstances change.

When selecting an index as a proxy for a money manager's performance, the main concern is whether it is representative of the manager's style and approach. Index creators have their own agenda. For example, some indexes may not be designed for the sole purpose of providing an effective benchmark for measuring the performance of money managers (or even as a proxy for plan fund fiduciaries to use when formulating investment policy). Individual country indexes are designed to fit nice and neatly into the macro-world indexes of the various index generators. However, not all country indexes do.

Determining the right benchmark and value-added target gives a "telltale" to the money manager; however, if not done properly, it can send the wrong message. As discussed in Chapter Three, if the value-added target is set too high, the money manager might assume that the client wants it to be more aggressive and might take larger bets to deliver the value-added results. This could result in the manager taking on more risk than what was intended by the client.

Determining the appropriate benchmark for measuring success or failure is neither an art nor a science. Most measurement tools have flaws; yet investment committees and investors make hire and fire decisions based on these benchmarks and/or peer-group placements. Untimely, firing, and inappropriate hiring, of money managers can be very costly. Selecting the benchmark and value-added target is as important as the management of the investment portfolio. The plan sponsor has to make sure that it sends the right message by selecting the appropriate benchmark and target.

The U.S. market is fairly efficient (however, not totally efficient). As a result, U.S. index/passive funds might provide a suitable alternative to active strategies. This might not be the case for other markets around the world. The more concentrated the index, the less likely it is to work as a substitute for active money management (i.e., in concentrated/less diversified markets it might be easier for managers to exploit market inefficiencies to create value-added results).

In summary, determining an effective, representative, relevant, and investable benchmark will assist in improved communication and understanding between the plan sponsor and the money manager. However, it should not be the sole, dominant driver of the manager selection decision-making process.

The members of an investment committee have a difficult and daunting task when it comes to measuring for success. As stated earlier, past performance of money managers might not be indicative of future performance. As well, the standards used to measure the performance of money managers may be flawed. I understand that performance measurement is a *must*. It is important that the plan sponsor, investment planning consultant, and money manager are all on the same page when setting the desired performance standards. As indicated in the previous chapter, recent poor performance may be one of the last reasons for firing a money manager.

CHAPTER SEVEN

TRADE COMMISSION DOLLARS

It Is Your Money

Just a thought:

A little while back I decided to try my hand at self-deprecation; however, after a few months, I had to give it up. I was just not very good at it.

INTRODUCTION

Commission dollars represent the cost of a broker/dealer executing security transactions, as directed by plan sponsors, or money management organizations operating on behalf of their clients.

Commission dollars are typically responsible for covering three primary activities of a broker/dealer:

1. the actual hard-dollar cost of the transaction itself (the pure execution cost);

2. proprietary research of the brokerage firm (and, in some cases, the research and services of third-party vendors); and,

3. the service coverage the broker/dealer provides to the money manager (e.g., keeping the money manager up-to-date on economic, industry, and company trends, on buy and sell orders within the marketplace, and new research ideas) and other services rendered by the brokerage firm (e.g., setting up meetings with corporate management).

Commission dollars are used by the money manager (with full or partial discretion from the plan sponsor) to execute trades within portfolios on behalf of the plan sponsor. In investment terms, any commission dollars above the pure execution cost are referred to as "soft dollars" or sometimes as "soft commissions".

Why do I devote an entire chapter to commission dollars? Commissions generated by the money manager and commission dollars directed by the plan sponsor for their own internal requirements create a situation in which these commission dollars can be misused. Commission dollars are the *sole* property and responsibility of the plan sponsor. As a result, conditions for their use must be addressed within the investment policy statement, or as a separate trade and commission allocation policy. One of the primary fiduciary responsibilities of the investment committee is to consider *all* costs of administering and managing a pension or investment fund. Reducing commission costs enhances overall fund returns (all things being equal) while, perhaps, lowering fund expenses.

The issue of soft dollars (how they are used, accounted for, and reported on) has haunted investment regulators for more than five decades. Regulators would like to find a way to do away with soft dollars, or at least to reduce their usage; however, the best they have been able to do is to create regulations or standards about the proper *use* of soft dollars by the regulated entities—asset managers, investment planning consultants, and brokers. Plan sponsors are not regulated in this regard; however, they are guided by their duty to act exclusively in the best interests of the plan participants and their beneficiaries. The use of soft dollars, directed commissions, and commission recapture programs by the investment community is very ingrained in the ecosystem of the investment world. Its elimination might significantly affect the basic functioning of the portfolio implementation process.

For *investment managers*, it may reduce the scope of research and other services available as input into the investment decision-making process. Use of soft dollars may eliminate a significant income source of *brokerage firms*—as a large portion of all equity trade commissions pays for their internal research costs. Eliminating soft-dollar usage may erode the access of *third-party vendors* to a revenue channel for payment of their unique product or service to assist investment managers in their decision-making process. Eliminating the use of soft dollars may also reduce the ability of *plan sponsors* and other investors to lower overall pension/investment-related costs, or the ability to receive additional income through a commission recapture program. Finally, *consultants* may not be able to set up directed commission arrangements with their clients, for which they receive a percentage of the commissions generated, or have their services paid for in soft dollars.

As commissions are the sole property of the plan sponsor, it is the responsibility of the investment committee members to address this issue and create a trade and commission allocation policy that outlines the plan sponsor's intended use of commission dollars.

SOFT DOLLARS DEFINED

CFA Institute's definition of soft dollars is consistent with the definitions of other overseeing regulatory bodies. According to CFA Institute Soft Dollar Standards, a soft dollar practice "refers to an arrangement whereby the Investment Manager directs transactions to a Broker, in exchange for which the Broker provides Brokerage and Research Services to the Investment Manager. Soft Dollar Arrangements include Proprietary and Third-Party Research Arrangements but do *not* include Client-Directed Brokerage Arrangements." Basically, any part of the commission dollar paid to a broker above the cost of pure execution is considered "soft"—covering the cost of proprietary research from the brokerage firm as well as any third-party research from other service providers that directly supports the manager's decision-making process.

There is no doubt that commission dollars generated by money managers and plan sponsors have often been used for entirely inappropriate purposes. Because of these past abuses, the term "soft dollars" often conjures up a negative association. Even when commissions are handled appropriately by all concerned, there is a preconception that someone is getting something for nothing, or vice versa.

THEIR PURPOSE

Paying out commission dollars is a cost of doing business. As with any other cost relating to administering and managing a pension or investment fund, there must be a policy that states how these commission dollars are to be used.

There are four primary uses of commission dollars:

1. *Trade execution*: Brokers are paid to initiate and complete buy and sell transactions for their clients (typically, the money manager responsible for the trade and, in some cases, the plan sponsor). For stocks, the commission for trading is calculated by quoting on a cents-per-share basis. On a straight execution basis, the price per share may be in the range of 1 to 1.5 cents. This is the purest of all commission payments, as it consists only of the cost of undertaking the transaction.

2. *Soft-dollar transactions*: Soft dollars, as addressed earlier, are commission costs over and above the actual cost of executing the trade itself. Any additional amount over the execution cost is typically allocated to investment research or related services exclusively for the use by the money managers in their decision-making process (and sometimes the plan sponsor in its role as a money manager). Investment research falls into two main categories: a) research generated from the transacting broker (proprietary research); and b) research provided by an outside vendor, with payment through the brokerage firm (third-party research). When investment research is brought into the equation, the cost of transacting goes up. The price per share now is in the region of 4 cents per share (depending on the size and nature of the stock transaction). As a result, excluding the actual cost of executing, the allocation of commission dollars to research and servicing accounts for somewhere between two-thirds and three-quarters of the total 4 cents per share. In the vast majority of cases, the money manager has sole discretion over the selection of the brokerage firm and the allocation of commission dollars.

3. *Client-directed commission arrangements*: Commissions may be *directed* by the plan sponsor specifically for its own use to cover the costs of certain dedicated resources required in administering and managing its own pension or investment fund. Some acceptable services for payment with directed commissions include actuarial or consulting services; specific economic, political, or social research reports as they relate to pension and investment fund activities; asset/liability studies; and performance measurement services. Once again, a policy addressing the proper use of commission dollars must be developed to show that the benefit is exclusive to the plan participants and their beneficiaries—and not for the benefit of the plan sponsor itself just to reduce overall costs of administering the pension or investment fund.

4. *Commission recapture programs:* As with directed commissions, a commission recapture programs falls under the authority and responsibility of the plan sponsor. Here, the plan sponsor sets up an account with its custodian and brokerage firm; the broker may *rebate* a portion of the commissions paid back to the fund to this account. From here, the money could be placed back into the fund as an additional income stream. These programs are sometimes referred to as "commission-rebate programs."

Investment committee members must address these uses of generated commissions and create a policy that reflects their beliefs and what is in the best interest of the fund participants.

THE PLAYERS

With the allocation of commission dollars there are as many as five primary parties involved.

The Plan Sponsor

Portfolio security transactions generate commissions—which, as indicated above, are a cost of doing business. As with any other expenditure from a fiduciary fund, these commission dollars must be used by the plan sponsor (or fund trustees, as the case may be) and the investment manager acting as an agent on behalf of its (their) client for the exclusive benefit of the fund participants and their beneficiaries. The plan sponsor must, therefore, address the usage of commission dollars. To do so, the plan sponsor has the following three options:

1. *Delegating full authority* to the investment manager(s) regarding trade execution—the most common arrangement.

2. *Setting guidelines* regarding the commission payments by the money manager to third-party service providers. For example, place a maximum commission allocation (either as a specified dollar amount or as a percentage of the total commissions generated over a specified time period) for all third-party research. Selecting a specific dollar amount as a target might force the money manager to be a more active trader to comply with the client's wishes. This is not the outcome that is beneficial to the fund participants.

3. *Directing payments* from commission dollars to pay for appropriate research or service requirements of the plan sponsor that are determined for the benefit of the beneficiaries (not the plan sponsor) or, providing an additional income stream to the fund itself.

If a plan sponsor decides to direct commissions for its own use, there are some issues to consider. Plan administrators can satisfy specific internal financial obligations (e.g., performance measurement services, custodial services, actuarial and pension consulting, and economic, political, and industry research studies/reports) by directing its money manager(s) to allocate trades to a specific participating brokerage firm—which would then use part of the commissions generated to pay for the required research or services of the plan sponsor. Again, any selected service must be for the sole benefit of the plan participants.

Note that directed commissions might not be able to be commingled with commissions of other clients. As a result, if a money manager has an opportunity to purchase a block trade at a discount price, the directed commission trade might not get the same attractive fill. A manager that is strongly encouraged to deal with a specific broker to fulfill an obligation to the plan sponsor might not obtain best execution on that specific trade, or might have to trade more frequently than necessary to satisfy the financial expectations of the plan sponsor.

If the plan sponsor permits soft-dollar transactions or directs commissions, then it should require the following information, at least annually, from the money manager:

1. a description of all soft-dollar research and services paid for from their portfolio;

2. how each service relates to the manager's decision-making process;

3. what percentage of total commissions paid from the client's trades or participation in blocks is attributed to research and other services, as opposed to pure execution;

4. the average commission rate paid for soft-dollar trades versus that paid for non-soft-dollar trades; and,

5. if applicable, what conversion ratio was negotiated by the consultant or investment manager to convert soft dollars into hard dollars.

For plan sponsors, one of the benefits of creating directed commission arrangements and commission recapture programs is that they are typically off-balance sheet items. Pension and investment costs can be covered without being part of the plan sponsor's budgetary process. However, the area has potential for abuse.

The Investment Manager

The investment manager has the fiduciary responsibility to seek "best execution" in all portfolio transactions—with the proviso that best execution is not necessarily defined as the lowest commission cost. As noted, commissions generated must be in the best interest of the beneficiary of the assets.

The various regulatory authorities permit commission dollars to be allocated for two activities: 1) trade execution, and 2) research. However, the vast majority of full-service brokerage firms still provide a bundled service (i.e., the plan sponsor and money manager have to guess what the split of the commission dollar is between execution and research/service—and it is likely to differ for each broker/dealer). As a result, investment managers generally cannot be fully aware of the exact cost of the specific research reports and analysis they receive—and, therefore, plan sponsors might not be able to determine whether the overall cost is acceptable.

There are three reasons that investment management firms may use soft-dollar transactions (outside of brokerage firms providing their own proprietary research):

1. to reduce their overall corporate operating costs;

2. to obtain research or services not readily available through traditional brokerage firms; and,

3. to appease clients that have set up directed commission arrangements or recapture programs.

Of these reasons, only the second is unequivocally an appropriate use.

In addition to access to a broker's proprietary research, investment managers may allocate soft dollars for a variety of other services (e.g., performance measurement services, portfolio modeling and technical analysis software, political/economic/social reports, computers and terminals, fundamental databases, third-party research, stock quote systems, pricing services, custodial services, market-oriented data, and proxy-voting services), all with the purpose of enhancing the manager's decision-making process (at least, it is supposed to work that way). For example, the investment management firm might pay for its Bloomberg terminals, either in whole or in part, if they are clearly needed in support of the firm's investment decision-making process.

As well, soft-dollar usage by investment managers results in a hidden cost of active management—hindering the efforts of the plan sponsor in evaluating the true cost of obtaining active portfolio management services. Plan sponsors that prohibit the use of soft dollars may be getting a free ride from the research and services paid for by the soft dollars of other investors. The money manager has shown that brokerage firms will accept a lower profit on a trade for the plan sponsor that allows the use of soft dollars. That is, if the cost for the money manager is 4 cents for trading a stock for both a client using soft dollars and a client not using soft dollars, then the net cost on the soft-dollar trade to the brokerage firm might be 3 cents a share; the client without this arrangement has paid 4 cents—or a premium of 1 cent per share. The brokerage firm actually was willing to take a lower profit on the soft-dollar trade. Should the plan sponsor that does not use soft dollars get a commission discount on all trades with that broker? For the money manager, it is very difficult to be fair to all clients when some permit the use of soft dollars and others do not.

Within an investment management firm, the allocation of commission dollars is generally determined by one or more of the portfolio managers, analysts, or traders—as it serves as a reward system to the broker/dealer. The allocation of commissions should be based on the ability of the brokerage firm to perform high-quality trade execution, the quality and value of its proprietary research and the third-party research provided, and the overall servicing capabilities of the brokerage firm (e.g., access to corporate management meetings and first call on a trade)—basically, placing trust in the people and firm to deliver valuable services.

The Broker/Dealer

As stated earlier in the chapter, the majority of brokerage firms offer a full-service platform to the investment management community consisting of three primary activities: 1) efficient execution of trades, 2) proprietary research, and 3) coverage and other services. Some full-service brokers permit the allocation of commission dollars to pay for third-party research and services for the money manager and/or plan sponsor. There may also be brokerage firms that will not accept soft-dollar trades. In addition, some brokerage firms (known as discount brokers) provide an execution-only service—although, even here, a portion of the commission dollars may go toward third-party vendors for services outlined in the earlier section under "Investment Manager."

The Third-Party Vendor

Third-party research and services definitely can be a benefit to money managers as a way to enhance their decision-making process by providing non-traditional and custom-designed research and services that are not offered through the traditional brokerage firm channels. In the case of third-party vendors, plan sponsors know exactly what they or their money manager are paying for—with the proper documentation.

The Consultant

Some consulting firms have developed a service for their clients that:

1. captures some of the commission dollars generated to pay for predetermined third-party services required by the plan sponsor (e.g., performance measurement and asset/liability studies);

2. creates an additional income stream through a commission recapture program, which places a portion of the commission dollars back into the account of the plan sponsor; and/or,

3. pays for the consultant's fees.

The consultant, through its clout, may develop a transactions allocation program directly with one or more brokerage firms for its client base. The money manager is then told of the arrangement and asked to allocate a predetermined portion of a trade (either a specific dollar amount or a percentage of total commission dollars generated by a client's portfolio) to this recapture program—usually with the caveat that it should be done on a "best efforts" basis. Whatever the source of the commission dollars available for recapture, the plan sponsor and investment manager should, before deciding whether to enter into this arrangement, compare this process against other means for achieving lower net commission costs, and then determine the potential for unsatisfactory execution or loss of relevant research to the investment manager.

Soft dollars and directed commissions in and of themselves are not evil. They have some benefits. They can enhance competition for non-traditional research and services by allowing independent research providers access to the money management community; giving managers more choices; and, they can help smaller money management firms by lowering the barriers to entry. However, there are concerns with the use of soft dollars. These arrangements might raise overall transaction costs, result in inefficient trading where fulfilling a commitment trumps best execution, and lead to money managers misallocated resources when purchasing marginal research and services.

The plan sponsor must address the following questions:

- Should the manager be permitted to use soft dollars? If so, what are the guidelines?

- Should the plan sponsor use directed commissions to pay for research or services that it believes are for the sole benefit of the plan participants? If so, what are these services?

- Should the plan sponsor set up a commission recapture program to create an additional income stream to the fund?

- Above all, how does the plan sponsor measure and evaluate the benefit to plan beneficiaries?

In summary, the appropriate use of every commission dollar starts with a well-thought-out and clearly expressed trade and commission allocation policy by the plan sponsor. From there, the plan sponsor should maintain a full understanding of how the plan sponsor's agents—primarily money managers—manage the commissions under their control. As well, an effective reporting, monitoring, and evaluation structure should be in place to ensure that commissions continue to be used by the plan sponsor and its agents in the most cost-effective way for the fund and to the benefit of all plan participants. CFA Institute Soft Dollar Standards sets out ethical principles that are designed to provide "full and fair disclosure" of soft-dollar trades, "consistent presentation of information" for understanding and clarification, "uniform disclosure and record keeping", and ensure "high standards of ethical practices within the investment industry."

Bottom line: The overall disadvantages of using soft dollars, directed commissions, and commission recapture programs may far outweigh the advantages. Yes, there are exceptions—but they are few. The potential for conflict may outweigh the advantages. It might not be worth the time and effort to gain a cent from a commission split at the expense of, say, a 25-cent potential trading loss per share by not getting the right fill. I have always had this one concern that plan sponsors pay the money managers twice: once with the management fees charged, and again when the money manager uses the plan sponsor's commission dollars to pay for services and products that could or should be paid for with their own monies out of their operating budget. It is the money managers generating commissions with the various brokerage firms that get invited to conferences in exotic locals—not the investment committee members.

Consistent with the theme of this book, plan sponsors and money managers are treated differently from the brokerage community due to the size of their assets under management and relationships. It is very difficult for plan sponsors to monitor the trading activities of their money managers to determine whether commission dollars are truly benefiting the fund participants. In addition, it is also difficult to determine best execution with all the parties involved and the complexities of each trade. Commission usage is just one more opportunity to game against the plan sponsor. There is a lot of trust involved here that all service providers are working in the best interests of the beneficiary. However, it is the fiduciary responsibility of the investment committee members to understand the process and put in place the required policy and monitoring procedures.

Refer to Appendix 6 for a sample trade and brokerage allocation policy.

CHAPTER EIGHT

INCENTIVE-BASED FEES

Is There a Winner?

Just a thought:

A few years ago, our 20th wedding anniversary was coming up and I had no idea what gift to get my wife. When I asked her what she would like for this anniversary, she said she wanted a divorce. I had to tell her I was not planning on spending that much.

INTRODUCTION

It has been just over 30 years since the introduction of performance-based fees in the U.S. In mid-November 1985, the Securities Exchange Commission (SEC) and other regulatory authorities removed the restrictions prohibiting investment managers from creating custom-designed fee arrangements based on performance results. This was a fairly easy decision for the SEC to make, as plan sponsors, the investment management community, and consulting organizations, in general, had been advocating for its removal—albeit for different reasons. On the one hand, plan sponsors felt that if the fund performed poorly against the criteria they set, then they should not have to pay full freight on management fees—as performance expectations were not achieved. On the other hand, investment managers believed that their stellar performance in the early 1980s had given them the opportunity to capitalize on their value-added results and extract more revenues from their existing client base—given a performance-based fee structure. In summary, plan sponsors wanted to reduce overall costs when things went bad, whereas money managers wanted to increase revenue when things went well. As well, consultants operating as intermediaries, between the plan sponsors and money managers would be able to create another service by creating performance-based fee structures. Everyone was happy. What could go wrong here?

INCENTIVE-BASED FEES DEFINED

For the remainder of this chapter, I eschew the popular term "performance-based fees" in favor of "incentive-based fees"—as I believe the latter term to be a more inclusive definition of what might be considered an "incentive" to deliver on return expectations (i.e., the fee structure might not be linked solely and purely to performance results).

In the money management community, there are three basic types of fee structures:

1. a *fixed-dollar* fee structure is generally set at the beginning of the relationship between the investment manager and the plan sponsor. It is a predetermined number and is not likely to vary based on the size of the assets under management or the performance of the portfolio;

2. the majority of money managers provide plan sponsors with an *asset-based* sliding fee structure based on the size of assets under management; as assets increase, the breaks in the fee scale come down (e.g., 50 basis points for a $10-million portfolio moving to 30 basis points for a $100-million portfolio), and so on (it pays to be big); and,

3. in an *incentive-based* fee structure, the management fees paid are adjusted based primarily on the level of performance against predetermined performance standards (typically, a specific market index, plus some value-added target). If performance is above the benchmark and value-added target (an amount to cover the cost of active management and perhaps the risk of going active), then the plan sponsor pays a higher fee (increasing the cost to the plan sponsor and increasing money manager revenue). If performance falls below the value-added target, the plan sponsor pays a lower

fee (reducing the management fee to the plan sponsor and reducing the revenue stream of the money manager).

Incentive-based fees are typically custom designed by the money manager for the plan sponsor, by the plan sponsor for the money manager, or by a third party (e.g., an investment planning consultant) for the plan sponsor, the money manager, or both. The consultant operates as an unbiased agent in the negotiations of the incentive-based fee structure—or, at least, that is how it should be.

In theory, from the perspective of the plan sponsor, an incentive-based fee structure provides a direct relationship between the performance delivered above the benchmark/value-added target over a predetermined timeframe, and the actual management fee that would be paid. The main objective is to reward the money manager for outperformance (however defined) and penalize the manager for underperformance.

An asset-based fee structure, as outlined earlier in this chapter, may also be considered an incentive-based fee, as it has a direct link to the asset base—if assets increase in value, the fees to the money manager also rise. As a result, any fee structure that is linked directly to historical performance can be considered an incentive-based fee. However, with the asset-based fee, the link to performance is not as strong as it is with an incentive-based fee.

The most important aspect of an incentive-based fee structure is to align the goals and objectives of the client with the money manager.

FROM THE PERSPECTIVE OF THE PLAN SPONSOR

The plan sponsor may propose an incentive-based fee structure for three reasons:

1. a belief that an incentive-based fee leads to better performance than would be expected without the incentive;

2. a belief that, should performance results fall below expectations, the money manager should *share* in this underperformance through lower fees; and,

3. possibly, the realization that plan sponsors do not have the skill or experience to select superior money managers and, therefore, are hedging their bets should the manager fail to deliver on performance expectations.

With respect to the belief that an incentive-based fee leads to improved performance, money managers are obligated to not favor one client over another within the same mandate—all clients must be treated fairly and equitably. From the viewpoint of the plan sponsor, an incentive-based fee is almost like a "bribe" to the money manager to put the plan sponsor's interests ahead of those of the money manager's other clients that do not have an incentive-based fee arrangement. If the incentive does not create an advantage over other clients, and if performance results beat the performance target, then the plan sponsor might be paying more for the same performance delivered to the other clients that do not have this arrangement.

With respect to the belief that the money manager should share in this underperformance through lower fees, when considering the money manager fee structure, the plan sponsor is *rewarded* for selecting an underperforming manager by paying a lower fee, and *penalized* for choosing a manager that outperformed the bogey by paying a higher fee. Our industry is strange.

The main concern for the plan sponsor is the impact that any incentive-based fee structure would have on the money manager's decision-making process and behavior. If the incentive-based fee is attractive enough to the money manager, with a significant anticipated reward, then it has the potential to influence the behavior of the money management organization. However, this outcome is what the plan sponsor is hoping for—if it puts them first. A problem for the plan sponsor is the lack of transparency and available information to adequately compare investment management fee arrangements from one manager to another, as well as what managers charge all their other clients for the same mandate.

With respect to the plan sponsor hedging their bets should the manager fail to deliver on performance expectations, if the plan sponsor or investment planning consultant does not have the ability and confidence to select superior managers, and the only goal of the plan sponsor is to pay lower fees, the plan sponsor should consider passive alternatives that typically have lower associated fees.

One last point that might be to the plan sponsor's benefit: incentive-based fees are typically based on the past performance of the money manager—given the historical value-added target they delivered above the designated index. As a result, if the manager had provided historical value-added results over the benchmark of, say, 200 basis points, the odds are reduced that those results would be replicated in the future—as competition, constantly evolving with new technology, increases with each decade. For the plan sponsor, the money manager might still add value against the benchmark—perhaps just not the 200 basis points.

FROM THE PERSPECTIVE OF THE MONEY MANAGER

This is a short discussion: the *only* reason for a money manager to either initiate an incentive-based fee structure or accept one from a plan sponsor or investment planning consultant is to increase revenues. Money managers are likely to only select incentive-based fee arrangements that are favorable to them. They have the in-depth experience and knowledge of their performance cycles. They would probably not initiate an incentive-based fee structure if it were not expected to be to their advantage. However, money managers are generally over-optimistic about their ongoing capabilities to add longer-term value-added results, and, as a result, incentive-based fees are typically less of a benefit to the manager than hoped for. This works in the favor of the plan sponsor, as there are major egos involved on the money management side. They typically believe that past performance can be replicated. Of course, the perception that the client might walk away if the money management firm does not accept the incentive-based fee arrangement proposed by the plan sponsor may be another reason for the manager to accept such fees.

The major negative for money management firms accepting incentive-based fees is that cash flows to the firm can fluctuate owing to over- and under-achievement in the portfolios. If performance is poor within a certain mandate, revenues would decline—and clients could terminate their relationships. The greater cyclicality with the revenue stream and profit base could result in turnover among senior, seasoned investment professionals (as their remuneration package might be reduced) or prohibit the money management organization from achieving its business planning objectives.

An incentive-based fee may be appropriate for portfolio mandates that are offered within niche areas of the marketplace (e.g., micro-cap stocks and below-investment-grade corporate bonds), where the illiquidity of the investment universe is finite and assets under management would have to be (or should be) capped at a certain level. An incentive-based fee provides the money manager with an opportunity to increase revenues without taking on more clients. However, these mandates should only be offered to *all* clients on the same fee structure.

STRUCTURING THE INCENTIVE-BASED FEE

Creating a fair and equitable incentive-based fee structure is quite difficult—there are a number of variables to consider. On the one hand, the plan sponsor is hoping that the optimal incentive-based fee arrangement results in performance results above what would be expected without an incentive-based fee structure in place. On the other hand, the money manager is hoping that its skills will continue to provide value-added returns, resulting in increased revenue.

Once decided, the incentive-based fee structure needs to address the following six primary components:

- *Normal* or *neutral* portfolio: This is a money manager's portfolio that is representative of the manager's investment style, approach and decision-making process for selecting securities—the universe from which securities are selected and any permanent tilts, biases, and/or factor bets.

- *Benchmark*: To be effective, the benchmark must come as close as possible to matching the neutral portfolio of the manager. It must be relevant, measurable, representative, investable, and replicable. The criteria for what constitutes a suitable benchmark was outlined in Chapter Six.

- *Value-added target*: This target reflects what would be a reasonable assumption for outperforming the benchmark—given the active decisions made by the money manager, and the fact that the incentive fee is based on an expected value-added return. For example, assume the benchmark is the S&P 500 Index with a value-added target of 100 basis points. If the manager exceeds this targeted return, the incentive-based fee calculation is triggered to reflect the manager's skill.

- *Time horizon*: A period that is appropriate for measuring the money manager's skill is the time horizon. The typical timeframe is three to five years; however, too short a time horizon may result in the plan sponsor rewarding luck rather than skill. A longer-term time horizon gives the money manager greater opportunity to game the system by either taking on more risk within the portfolio to make up for lost ground if performance suffers, or becoming more benchmark-like and reducing the benchmark risk level of the portfolio to lock in the current value-added gains.

- *Base Fee/limitations*: The most contentious issue tends to be agreeing on what the base fee should be. There are three main options to setting the base fee: first, selecting the fee that the plan sponsor would pay for an equivalent portfolio managed on a passive basis; second, determining the breakeven cost of doing business within the money management firm and setting this as the base fee—to cover the manager's general expenses so as not to be a loss-leader for the firm; and third, providing a discount to the manager's existing fee schedule—perhaps 20% below the posted fee schedule. The base fee also depends on the product or mandate and the investment style and approach of the money manager selected.

- *Fee parameters*: Fair and equitable fee parameters for the plan sponsor and money manager are determined by a *cap* on management fees on the upside (protecting the plan sponsor from paying too much) and a *floor* on fees on the downside (protecting the money manager).

PERCEIVED ADVANTAGES AND DISADVANTAGES

As with most activities within the investment management field, incentive-based fees have their advantages and disadvantages—and these will vary whether for a plan sponsor or an investment manager.

For the Plan Sponsor

Perhaps the main advantage of incentive-based fees for the plan sponsor is that they provide some comfort. If the money manager does not meet expectations, the plan sponsor could tell itself that despite selecting an underperforming money manager, at least it had saved money on fees.

As stated earlier in this chapter, the primary purpose of creating an incentive-based fee structure should be to align the client's and manager's interests. The time and effort to design the most effective and efficient fee structure forces both parties to understand the objectives and goals of the fund clearly. Both parties benefit from greater knowledge obtained during the process of determining the benchmark, value-added target, timeframe, etc.

Other advantages of incentive-based fees for the plan sponsor are:

1. if the plan sponsor believes that the incentive will create a higher return for the portfolio, it gives the plan sponsor a means to reward above-average results;

2. the willingness by the investment manager to accept an incentive-based fee structure could demonstrate that the manager is confident in its ability to generate the return expected;

3. for investment mandates that focus on less liquid market areas, the manager could put a limit on the size of the assets it will manage within the mandate to continue to deliver value-added results without compromising the integrity of the manager's investment style, approach, and bets; and,

4. an incentive-based fee could result in the money manager and the client sharing the risk of poor performance—comforting the plan sponsor that its money managers did the best they could, given the market conditions.

The primary disadvantage of incentive-based fees to the plan sponsor is that a fair and equitable incentive-based fee structure might not exist for either party. Unfortunately, the fairness might not be recognized for a very long time—and only after the fact.

Other disadvantages include:

1. an incentive-based fee structure depends heavily on accurate performance measurement, determining the normal portfolio, selecting the appropriate benchmark and value-added target, getting the time horizon right, agreeing on the base fee, etc.; getting all this right is difficult;

2. if the manager performs to expectations, the expenses of the plan sponsor increase (however, this is hopefully the result the plan sponsor was anticipating);

3. there is more time and effort spent on monitoring the structure—therefore, there may be an additional administration cost if not undertaken by the plan sponsor internally;

4. as plan sponsors have different goals and objectives, incentive-based fees are typically custom designed; as a result, there may be different incentive-based fee structures on the same product or mandate—perhaps providing greater incentive for one client over another; and,

5. as stated earlier, incentive-based fees could result in the manager gaming the process by taking greater risk when underperforming the target and reducing risk when outperforming the target—and locking in the gains.

Perhaps the greatest uncertainty is determining whether the plan sponsor is paying for luck or skill. However, attempting to determine the skill of a money manager is the same whether there is an incentive-based fee structure or not. If skill cannot be determined, then a plan sponsor is placing all its hope that luck will rule the day.

For the Investment Manager

As stated, the primary advantage for the money manager is an increase in its revenue stream—if it can deliver on expectations.

Other advantages for the money manager of initiating or accepting an incentive-based fee structure include:

1. there is increased interaction between the client and investment manager—any opportunity to gather more information on the client's risk/reward profile is a good thing;

2. incentive-based fees may result in a money manager seeking out every option possible to increase the return of the portfolio; and,

3. if the money manager's skill is consistent over time, and targets are met, it may result in the manager having higher revenues to reinvest back into the business—adding additional resources to maintain value-added results.

As indicated earlier, the main disadvantage for the investment manager is created by the volatility in the revenue stream that may arise from falling short of performance targets. This could result in business uncertainty—a chance of bankruptcy or investment professional turnover when compensation packages are reduced. Also, incentive-based fees may eventually result in tensions between the plan sponsor and money manager, as it might prove awkward to ask the client to write a bigger check if performance was significantly greater than what might have been anticipated.

As noted earlier in the chapter, only two situations may warrant an incentive-based fee structure: first, when the incentive-based fee is for the whole mandate or fund and is the same for all clients that are in the mandate or fund—the plan sponsor knows the rules and all clients are treated fairly and equitably; and second, incentive-based fees may be appropriate for mandates that operate in niche or illiquid areas of the marketplace. The money manager may believe they can capture value-added results only by keeping the assets under management in this mandate to a set maximum. With an incentive-based fee structure, the money manager would be rewarded for achieving a return above the benchmark target. As with the first point, all clients should have the same fee arrangement.

In summary, the investment committee members must consider the following points if they wish to implement an incentive-based fee structure:

1. it is very difficult (however, not impossible) to set up an arrangement that is fair and equitable to both parties over time—there are many moving parts (e.g., determining the neutral portfolio of the manager; selecting the most appropriate benchmark; setting the acceptable value-added target for both parties; picking the right time period for performance measurement, ensuring performance results are accurately calculated; and, determining the most appropriate base fee to use—including the cap and the floor);

2. the premise from the perspective of a plan sponsor is that the money manager will try harder. However, hopefully, the professional

managers selected will always do their very best to achieve the goals and objectives the plan sponsor has set out, without any additional incentives. As stated, there is already a built-in incentive to do well, as when a money manager performs above expectations, assets increase, and, since fees are typically based on assets under management, fees also increase (moreover, there is always the incentive of not being fired for poor results); and,

3. if there are only a few clients with an incentive-based fee structure in the mandate selected, the additional incentive might prove detrimental to the plan sponsor and the other clients on the standard fee structure in that mandate.

In a partnership with the money management organization, it is more important to match complementary cultures (e.g., mission, beliefs, and values) than to focus on the financial incentives designed to make the money manager try harder.

Some final thoughts:

- Plan sponsors that have incentive-based fee structures might pay significantly more in fees if the money manager achieves the desired outperformance with all its other clients with the same mandate without the added incentive—if these incentives-based fees do not change the manager's mindset.

- Historical returns are not a predictor of future results. If historical returns have been exceptional, linking the manager to an outperformance target that might never be achieved in the future would result in the client paying less than the standard fee schedule—a benefit to the plan sponsor. The whole process assumes that value-added results are repeatable over the longer term.

- An incentive-based fee structure should not provide an incentive for the money manager to favor one client, or client type, over another; nor should it provide an opportunity for the manager to game against the structure by taking more risk or less risk within the portfolio. However, the potential is there. With plan sponsors who do not have or want an incentive-based fee structure, the plan sponsor should know if any other clients in the mandate they have chosen have this fee structure, and how this has worked for the other clients within this mandate.

- Incentive-based fees focus almost exclusively on the return component of performance with little regard for risk.

- If the stock market has dropped by 20%, and the portfolio has declined by only 10%, would a plan sponsor be happy to pay more in incentive fees as the manager outperformed the performance target, despite the 10% lost on the fund's assets?

- Only in hindsight would a plan sponsor be able to judge whether the structure was fair and equitable. Typically, only one party turns out to be happy (except for the consultants—they are always happy).

In summary, an incentive-based fee structure sounds great in theory—providing a carrot to encourage more time and effort in the decision-making process to deliver even better performance. But does it work well in practice? If investment committee members enter into an incentive-based fee arrangement with their money managers, they must do this with their eyes wide open.

As with the overall theme of this book, I am not in favor of any incentives that result in one client's interest being placed ahead of another's.

CHAPTER NINE

SOME FURTHER ISSUES FOR CONSIDERATION

Not Finished Yet

Just a thought:

In going through life, the only certainty
I have found is that people entering a washroom have
the right of way over people coming out.

INTRODUCTION

The one thing that can be counted on in the investment management community is the number of topics up for discussion and debate at any given time. This chapter will address some specific issues and topics that should be addressed by the investment committee members when establishing an investment program.

ACTIVE STRATEGIES VERSUS PASSIVE APPROACHES

The most consistent ongoing debate within the investment community is that of *active* strategies versus *passive/index-matched* approaches. This debate has been raging since the first index fund was set up in the early 1970s. As each year passes, active management is slowly (maybe not too slowly) losing ground to passive approaches (at least in the more efficient markets—specifically, large-cap U.S. equity and core bond mandates). Passive approaches used to be the default to active management when active managers failed to meet their objectives. More and more, passive approaches are being considered as the first line of defense—with niche active strategies added around passive anchors or cores when active management is proven as an attractive alternative or complement.

The debate mainly centers on whether markets, in general, are efficient. However, no market is truly efficient—the issue is more the degree to which it is efficient (or inefficient). The U.S. market is the most efficient market in the world. Since the 1990s, studies have shown time and time again that the majority of active U.S., large-cap equity managers consistently underperform the S&P 500—yet the majority of large-cap equity assets in the U.S. continue to be actively managed with the S&P 500 as the benchmark. There are really true believers out there. Incidentally, these studies show that this persistent underperformance is evident even before considering the fees of active management. When fees are included, the percentage of alpha-challenged money managers moves higher.

Perhaps the reason that passive does not dominate in U.S. equity core-like portfolios is that plan sponsors may believe that the decision to go passive is an all-in decision. It is not. If the investment management structure includes equity management by region (e.g., U.S., Europe, Asia, and emerging markets), the U.S. component could be passive while the other regions, if proven that equity managers in those regions can achieve value-added results above their management fees, could have active strategies. In addition, money managers operating within the domestic markets may have an edge through their decision-making process or a specific concentration within a market segment that would complement a passive core. Another reason for selecting active is, perhaps, the overconfidence of the investment committee members with their consultants in their belief that they have the experience and skill to select managers that can consistently provide value-added results over longer periods of time.

In the active versus passive decision, one consideration is the intangible aspects of going active. With active management, there must be a long due-diligence process in selecting the right active money managers. As stated in Chapter Two, investment committee members might not have the education, experience, skills, and, perhaps, time to select active managers effectively. This leaves the valuation process up to the investment planning consultant, and, as pointed out earlier in Chapter Four, these consultants have their own built-in biases and conflicts.

It is easy to determine the cost advantage of passive versus active on a pure fee basis—one simply subtracts passive fees from active fees. As a result, fees for passive alternatives might be some 10 to 50 basis points lower (or more)—depending on the specific mandate. However, there are also some hidden costs when going the active route, including:

1. time and effort costs for the investment committee members;

2. out-of-pocket expenses if traveling to the money manager's offices;

3. the cost of portfolio transitioning (brokerage commissions plus market impact), if replacing an existing active manager with another active manager; and,

4. continual monitoring of results and regular meeting updates—with passive approaches, there is no need to go to the manager's office, and very little reason for meetings.

Bottom line: The decision to go active or passive is not an either/or decision. It depends on the beliefs of the plan sponsor, the efficiencies of the various components of the capital market, and the overall performance results and risk levels. As mentioned previously, the more diversified the specific individual market, the more likely it is to be more efficient, and, therefore, a passive approach might be more appropriate.

INTERNAL VERSUS EXTERNAL MANAGEMENT

The trend since the 1980s has been toward having pension and investment funds (or at least some portion of these funds) managed in-house. The main reason for this trend is the growth in pension and other institutional-type assets since 1970—both corporate pension funds and public sector funds.

As mentioned earlier, internally managed funds can have certain advantages. If the fund has unique goals or investment constraints, it might be easier for these specific issues to be addressed with an internal investment staff that has the necessary education, skills, and investment-related experience. Another advantage relates to risk management. A well-designed investment program could place more emphasis on risk acceptance or avoidance with better control procedures—the plan sponsor understands its own risk appetite. In addition, internal staff may be able to react more quickly to perceived market extremes in order to adjust the risk level of the fund, or to readjust the asset mix given a change in the plan characteristics. One main advantage that the mega funds have is their ability to establish internal investment teams to manage non-traditional asset classes (e.g., private equity, infrastructure, and hedge funds) that are custom designed for the fund as a whole. One last advantage is the ability of the plan sponsor to know, to the cent, the exact cost of administering and managing the investment program. There might also be a cost advantage.

Perhaps the greatest challenge to the plan sponsor when deciding to bring assets in-house is creating a remuneration structure that attracts the investment experience and skills required—as well as designing a nurturing culture to train, motivate, evaluate, and retain this talent. The plan sponsor will have to be competitive with the outside marketplace; however, given the all-in costs of talented investment professionals, the total remuneration packages might be difficult to swallow given the remuneration structures for the other divisions within the plan sponsor organization. As a result, some of the very large pension and investment funds separate out their investment management functions into stand-alone firms.

The main advantage of having investment funds externally managed is the choices available to the plan sponsor. At the asset mix level, smaller and mid-size pension and investment funds have pretty much the same opportunities and access to all the same asset classes as the mega funds—either through separately managed accounts, commingled fund vehicles, or bundled investment management platforms. The mega funds, with internal staff, are more likely to focus on one investment style or approach, whereas smaller pension and investment funds can diversify by combining complementary investment style offsets as a further means of diversification within an asset class. Another advantage of having the funds externally managed is the ability to fire money managers if they do not live up to expectations. It may be more difficult to fire an investment specialist or team within an organization if there are more personal corporate connections with the individuals or team.

Bottom line: All funds have pretty much the same options for asset classes when the focus is on diversification. On the return side, the mega funds may have a slight advantage at the total fund level, as they may have an opportunity to custom design private equity structures and infrastructure investments for the exclusive use of their own funds. On the risk side, internal management is unlikely to have an advantage over external management as the overall risk is managed at the asset mix level. The cost element is the other side of the equation. If the mega funds add extra value is it justified by the overall cost of the internal investment program?

Again, size is the main determinant in the decision to bring or retain the assets in-house.

DOES THE SIZE OF THE MONEY MANAGEMENT ORGANIZATION MATTER?

An ongoing question is whether pension and investment funds are better off being managed by large financial institutions or independent, boutique investment firms. The answer is: yes and no.

The advantages of a large money management organization include:

1. A large organization can build an in-depth internal staff of investment professionals with the ability to provide extensive research coverage whether within the domestic market or on a global basis.

2. A large investment management organization has economies of scale when it comes to dealing with the brokerage community. Given the amount of trading volume they can generate, they

are likely to get first call on investment ideas from the various brokerage firms. Furthermore, they are likely to be at the lower range of the commission scale.

3. Given the resources at their disposal, larger firms may be able to provide assistance with various studies that are of interest to plan sponsors without charging extra—products, information, and data that a consultant may charge for.

4. The depth and breadth of a large money management organization's servicing platform (e.g., fully dedicated specialists) may provide greater understanding of how the portfolio has achieved its returns. However, on the negative side, portfolio bets may be smaller, as larger financial institutions might have no other choice but to invest in highly liquid securities. Due to size, their universe for selecting securities might be restrictive.

The advantages of smaller money management firms include:

1. Smaller organizations have the potential ability to move in and out of the market without significantly affecting the price of the security.

2. The implementation process may be quicker in smaller firms with fewer hierarchies; larger organizations may have a longer process due to constraints placed on the decision-making structure with a more bureaucratic approval process.

3. The plan sponsor likely has access to the portfolio manager when and as required (which might not be the case with very large firms).

4. The universe for security selection of the mandate is likely wider than for larger firms (e.g., the universe for smaller money management firms may include mid-cap and small-cap stocks).

However, smaller firms are more vulnerable to disruptions. If the firm had only one asset class or investment style, it might be negatively affected by a steep market decline (affecting revenue), poor performance (resulting in a loss of clients and assets), and the loss of key investment professionals (a reputational issue).

There are pros and cons to choosing both larger money management organizations and smaller, independent boutique firms. There is probably less risk associated with selecting a large organization (e.g., their portfolios are well diversified and, therefore, the risk exposure might be lower; also, there is perceived to be safety in numbers). Meanwhile, smaller firms can move in and out of the market more quickly with less market impact, and can make larger bets—which may result in smaller firms having greater opportunity and potential to deliver alpha above the benchmark.

The culture within money management firms also plays a role in the choice. Larger firms tend to be more bureaucratic while smaller firms tend to be more entrepreneurial. However, this may not always the case.

The return potential of smaller money management organizations may override the economies of scale and lower overall risk of larger money management firms. Smaller firms are more aligned as investment management firms, whereas larger firms focus more on asset gathering. Money managers should be hired for their ability to deliver value-added results—if they can be found.

MANAGER COMPENSATION STRUCTURE

Over the years, through interviewing and analyzing slews of money management organizations in my role as an investment planning consultant, I have come across many types of compensation arrangements—for investment professionals within financial institutions versus independent investment management firms; for public investment management firms versus private investment management firms; for firms that have one shareholder versus firms whose multiple shareholders are spread throughout the organization; and for firms that use equity ownership as a main motivator versus firms that have "phantom" stock or profit-sharing plans as the main incentive structure—and I have yet to find a compensation structure that is truly in the best interests of the plan sponsor.

In money managers' marketing brochures and pitches, plan sponsors are told that the compensation structure chosen by the money management organization has been carefully designed to attract, motivate, and retain the top investment professionals in the country (or the world). However, in reality, the remuneration structure has been carefully designed to make the investment professionals rich.

What the plan sponsor would like to see is a structure that guarantees longevity for the money management firm (ensuring that the reins pass from one generation to another). However, longevity does not appear, on average, to work for independent investment management firms with pure equity ownership, either with one owner or spread throughout the organization, or with phantom stock or a well-designed profit-sharing plan, as these firms are created mainly as partnerships and generally have a finite life (typically, not much longer than 20 or so years). It does not seem to matter whether the investment management firm is public, as these firms continue to be bought out—and cease to exist. Investment professionals within financial institutions continue to leave their organizations—as owning 25% equity interest in a new independent firm is more lucrative and fulfilling than having a 2% ownership stake in a large financial institution.

Bottom line: There is no one magic compensation structure that guarantees that a plan sponsor's money manager will be around longer than the investment committee members. Partners/owners do not sell their money management firms based on what is in the best interests of the clients, but on what is best for the partners/owners themselves—it is human nature to focus on self-preservation and self-interest. Now, I know this perspective seems very cynical; however, the point is not to focus exclusively on how the investment professionals earn their keep. There is no one "right" remuneration package. The plan sponsor should aim to focus on how the money management firm aligns itself with its mission, beliefs, values, and goals and objectives. Succession planning may be more important than compensation from the perspective of the plan sponsor. As stated earlier, a written succession plan should be in place.

HOLDING COMPANY STOCK

Holding company stock within a pension or investment fund is not as prevalent today as it used to be; however, it still occurs in some cases. A corporate plan sponsor may have an ulterior motive for insisting that the fund hold company stock (e.g., to keep some share ownership out of public hands in case of an unwanted takeover offer). However, the corporate plan sponsor may even believe that its company stock is super attractive versus other stock alternatives, and may believe it is doing the fund beneficiaries a huge favor by including its stock in the fund. However, company stock inclusion within pension and investment funds directed by the plan sponsor results in an additional risk level for the fund beneficiaries—as both their livelihood and their retirement are linked to the company's fortunes. In the past, plan sponsors have not been very good judges of the intrinsic value of their own stock against others in the marketplace. They are basically more optimistic and overconfident about the prospects of their firm than those of their competition—they tend to extrapolate past results.

Stock inclusion places the investment committee members in a precarious position, as one of the tests they have to meet in their role as a fiduciary is to ensure appropriate diversification. The investment committee is now acting in the role of a money manager with a section of the fund it has no control over. This is a tough decision for the plan sponsor. There is the potential conflict of interest. Once again, the role of the investment committee members is to administer in the best interests of the plan beneficiaries.

THE ROLE OF THE CONSULTANT

Throughout this book, I have not been very complimentary about investment planning consultants. It has less to do with the individual consultants within the consulting firm and more to do with my concern regarding the specific culture of most of the investment planning organizations regarding: 1) their focus on billable hours or projects that are determined by and based on billable hours; and 2) the inherent biases that occur when these firms provide advice (e.g., asset mix studies and asset/liability models), services (e.g., manager searches, performance measurement), and investment products (e.g., money management platforms or providing outsourcing for the chief investment function). All three of these activities provide a significant conflict of interest—the firms are conflicted about what business they are in, while clients and prospective clients are not sure which hat the investment planning consultant is wearing when they seek the consultant's assistance.

However, given the concerns raised above, the role of the consultant is extremely important when setting up the governance structure for the administration and management of the investment fund. Yes, there are very good consultants and not-so-good consultants, as with any other professional group—and determining which is which typically results in a process of elimination. One of the themes of this book is that size matters. Larger plan sponsors likely have access to the top consulting specialists (i.e., more experienced professionals) within these organizations. As usual, the more money there is to dole out, the higher up the food chain the plan sponsor can go.

One of the benefits of using investment planning consultants is that they work with a variety of plan sponsors and other investment types with different focuses and demands. As a result, consultants are generally always on a learning curve—driven by their clients' thirst for knowledge. Larger plan sponsors with very large asset pools are typically ahead of consultants regarding trends that will affect their specific situation. As a result, consultants are more reactive to the needs of clients. For example, when hedge fund managers began to emerge in the late 1980s and early 1990s, consultants were slow to understand how they fit into the investment management structure and the overall benefit to the risk/reward profile of the fund. The larger clients of these consulting firms put pressure on the consultants to provide in-depth research on these new arrivals (as these hedge funds brought a new, deeper, richer meaning to the word "complexity").

Consulting firms can offer their services on a retainer-type basis (e.g., for continuing ongoing advice), a fee-for-service basis (e.g., performance measurement services) that is charged out periodically (generally, quarterly), or on a project-by-project basis (e.g., for an asset/liability study or manager search). The major benefit of a retainer-type relationship for the plan sponsor is the ability to have its consultants on speed dial should it require a study, information, or advice. In addition, consultants are able to get closer to their clients than they would otherwise—being more proactive to their needs. The challenge is for the plan sponsor to ensure that its ongoing requirements in value-added terms justify the retainer fee charged. Unlike the money management community, with its set fee schedule for each and every mandate, there is no set fee structure for a consulting firm's various services. They normally charge what the market will bear. As a result, consultant fees can vary significantly among consulting firms, and between the consulting firm's clients. Fees can sometimes be negotiated. The plan sponsor should ensure that whatever service it requires from the consultant organization is priced out in detail at the onset for ease of understanding. Again, one of the responsibilities of the fiduciary is to be aware of, and to control, the overall operating expenses of the investment program.

The last benefit of having a consultant is the added advantage of having someone to blame if things go wrong.

There is no doubt that the consulting community has significant conflicts of interest as well as biases in advising plan sponsors. However, a good consultant respects the needs of the plan sponsor, whether for advice, a service, or delivering an all-inclusive, packaged money management platform.

EXCLUSION AND INCLUSION

As stated many times in this book, prudence is primarily defined by the extent of diversification within a pension or investment fund. However, there are five distinct areas in which the investment committee members, at their discretion, could have an impact on diversification in an investment fund. Of these areas, three result in securities being in the *exclusion* category, and two fall into the *inclusion* category. Every time an investment committee sets rules for fund exclusion or inclusion, it creeps closer and closer to acting like a money manager with some direct accountability for overall fund performance.

There are basically three restrictions an investment committee can place on the investment fund that may exclude certain stocks or companies and reduce the potential for full objective diversification. The first involves "social justice" considerations. As an example, in 1977, the six (later, seven) Sullivan Principles were established in an attempt to influence social injustice in South Africa—which was ruled at the time by the National Party apartheid government. These principles were adopted, first, by some major universities, foundations, and charitable organizations, and, later, by government-type investment programs and some corporations to put economic pressure on the apartheid government. Pension and operating and endowment funds would exclude from their investments public companies that were operating in South Africa and that did not support the Sullivan Principles. After some court challenges, investment funds were permitted to make exceptions to full diversification requirements by the regulators.

The second restriction occurs when the investment committee eliminates the holding of its own company stock owing to a perceived conflict of interest. And the third restriction occurs when eliminating securities within certain industries (e.g., tobacco, alcohol, weapons, nuclear, and gambling) due to their negative impact on society—all resulting in further reducing the potential for full diversification.

There are also two main areas for including certain stocks or funds that can impact diversification. First, company stock can be included at the plan sponsor's own discretion. Second, companies that fall into the category of "social responsibility" can be actively included. In this case, the investment committee may decide to include a commingled fund that is designed to hold only securities of companies that meet the plan sponsor's definition of being socially responsible.

I understand the pressure that plan beneficiaries or other outside influencers may place on the plan sponsor to be socially responsible by, for example, eliminating "sin" stocks, or engaging in companies that pass the tests of being good corporate citizens with the appropriate governance procedures. However, how far down the food chain does the investment committee go? Does it eliminate financial institutions that lend money to the companies on the "naughty" list? Does it eliminate companies that supply bottles to companies manufacturing alcohol? The list may never end. The original list started with just tobacco.

I attempt to be a purist. I believe that if the investment committee members have delegated investment authority and responsibility over security selection to a money manager, then the manager should be given full discretion to invest in securities that will provide for appropriate diversification through an effective risk/reward trade-off. The good news is that money management firms are beginning to incorporate social investing within their security selection process. Also, it is sometimes difficult for investment committees to come to a consensus on what should be excluded or included. Committee members may have differing opinions. Social investing should be addressed in the beliefs of the plan sponsor.

MONEY MANAGEMENT CULTURE

It is very difficult to uncover and understand the culture of a money management firm from the outside looking in. If the plan sponsor asks, most investment professionals in money management firms, even those who had been with the company for at least 10 years, might have a difficult time describing the firm's culture.

Culture is determined by the professional leaders and the beliefs, values, and behavior they set in motion. It is also difficult to maintain a culture in an ever-changing investment environment, and culture can change significantly as investment professionals enter and exit the firm.

One major telltale of an investment management culture is the design and implementation of the reward system for the investment professionals within the organization. The remuneration structure sends a powerful message to the organization's staff about the focus and priorities of the investment management organization. There are four main areas or distinct divisions within an investment management organization:

- *investment management* (e.g., portfolio managers, strategists, economists, analysts, and traders);

- *marketing*;
- *servicing*; and,
- the *infrastructure* to support the first three levels.

The question is whether the reward system is tilted toward the investment professionals (as earning the anticipated rate of return is the primary goal), marketing and sales personnel (where adding new clients and assets is the main focus), or servicing specialists (where ongoing client satisfaction and retention are most important). Money managers typically prepare five-year business plans. The plan sponsor should ask how much money will be reinvested back into the firm each year, and the percent allocation to each of the four areas mentioned above.

For money management organizations that provide active strategies, the investment committee members' focus almost always comes down to the people. The characteristics we are told to look for in investment professionals include vision, confidence, basic intelligence and knowledge, ethical behavior, imagination, emotional stability, passion, a good work ethic, strong values, honesty, creativity, openness to new ideas, objectivity, a high degree of integrity, continuous learning, ability to communicate, flexibility, adaptability, high energy levels, curiosity, etc. However, as an outside observer looking in, it is virtually impossible to recognize and rate any of these characteristics for any of the investment professionals that the investment committee is considering to manage its fund. Again, how do you assess the firm's level of integrity? The final evaluation always comes down to personal judgment—one's own best guess. This is where the "art" comes into play.

Bottom line: Culture is all about the people—and the main test is how they are rewarded. Is their compensation scheme aligned with the beliefs and values of the plan sponsor? Culture is also about reinvesting in the organization—where is the money going?

CHAPTER TEN

THE ENDGAME

A Recap and Some Final Thoughts

Just a thought:

One requirement of surviving in our industry is the ability to understand trends and their impact on future events. I actually got pretty good at it. For example, I was the first to predict the sequel to the Walt Disney movie, The NeverEnding Story. *As an aside, I also don't understand the concept of movie prequels—it just seems like poor planning on the part of Hollywood.*

INTRODUCTION

The role of the investment committee is to set up efficient and effective processes and procedures to administer and manage pension and investment funds. Within most corporations, the investment committee should be considered the second most important committee (only after the board of directors), given its influence and impact on the lives of the corporation's employees. For all other organizations that have investment funds to administer and manage, the investment committee is likely the most important committee. After all, the funds are managed for the vast majority of beneficiaries within these organizations—what could be more important than assuring employees that they have an affordable lifestyle to look forward to in retirement?

The investment committee members have their work cut out for them. They face many challenges, including:

- understanding and accepting their role as a fiduciary;

- formulating asset mix policy in ever-changing pension, investment, and market environments;
- determining which asset classes will provide the return required to deliver on the promises made within an acceptable risk tolerance;
- setting out beliefs on whether active strategies or passive approaches are the most appropriate;
- providing a framework for selecting money managers and how they will collectively fit within the investment management structure;
- creating the necessary controls, processes, and procedures to monitor all investment activities constantly for continued success;
- determining which investment vehicles offer the best fit; and,
- keeping up with the regulatory environment and trends within the pension and investment markets.

The task is a difficult one; however, there is no other choice. Investment committee members *must* operate in a prudent manner—as experts would.

A RECAP

- *Beliefs:* As stated above, the investment committee is one of the most important committees (if not *the* most important committee) within a plan sponsor, investor, or other organization entrusted with the management of fund assets. The education and skills to administer and manage a pension or investment fund effectively and efficiently are not commonly found within plan sponsor organizations. Investment committee members cannot fulfill their fiduciary responsibility without members who are experienced in investment matters and able to select the appropriate service providers. The whole process starts with the investment committee's beliefs—its members should determine what is required for the fund's specific circumstances. It is likely that beliefs will change over time. Every three to five years, the investment committee should re-examine its stated beliefs, given the plan characteristics and the market environment, to ensure that they still represent the tenets to achieve the goals and objectives.

- *Prudence*: The investment committee members should remember that the fund is not theirs to play with. It is for the sole benefit of the fund beneficiaries (both current and retired). As a result, prudence must drive the decision-making process. Investment committees are there to provide oversight and to act in good faith.

- *Time:* The timeframe is important. The advantage of most pension funds is their long-term nature. Other types of investment funds (e.g., operating and endowment funds, and foundations) might not have the same luxury of time. The longer the foreseeable time horizon, the more predictable the returns (i.e., the closer they will come to the longer-term averages). Investment committee members should use time to their advantage—it may be their best friend.

- *Investment Policy Statement:* A primary responsibility of an investment committee is formulating an in-depth and meaningful investment policy statement. One of its goals is to outline the roles, responsibilities, and authorities of investment committee members as well as all the various service providers connected to the fund.

- *Committee Membership:* Investment committee membership should be contained to between three and eight members to be functional. Term limits should be established when, and if, possible. The investment committee requires an effective and knowledgeable chairperson to determine what is required on an ongoing basis to ensure that plan beneficiaries are placed first above all else.

- *Asset Mix Policy:* The most important decision the investment committee will make for the longer-term returns of the fund and the acceptable risk tolerance is to determine what asset classes and asset class segments to include within the fund's investment management structure. The most important factor is that asset mix policy will dominate (by far) any other factors affecting the return outlook and the risk tolerance. The decision to get right is the allocation between ownership-type assets and fixed-income assets. When considering alternative-type investments, the following points should be kept in mind: they are relatively new with a short-term performance history; higher fees are associated with these asset classes; they are less liquid and are not typically traded on public exchanges; they are less transparent—an observer might not be able to tell if things are going wrong; some funds can be wound up without notice; and they are perceived to be higher risk. However, they are also good diversifiers—as they have low correlations with traditional asset classes.

- *Gaming Against You:* Not everyone is a friend to the investment committee. Most (if not all) service providers to the pension and investment programs have conflicts of interest or, at the very least, potential conflicts of interest, given their self-interest, self-motivation, and self-preservation. Their goals and objectives are likely to clash with those set out by the investment committee. It is difficult, if not virtually impossible, to eliminate all of these conflicts. The investment committee members just have to be aware that these conflicts of interest do exist and to determine their impact on the fund as a whole. Basically, can the investment committee live with these conflicts?

- *Manager Selection:* One of the most time-consuming functions of the investment committee is hiring, monitoring, and then firing money managers—only to restart the process of hiring all over again. The first decision to be made (based on the investment committee's beliefs and experience) is whether to go the active route or rely on passive/index-matched alternatives. This is not an either/or decision, as it depends on the markets in which the fund is invested and the investment committee's views about whether active solutions have the potential to achieve the fund's goals, given the value added versus the overall costs of being active. If the active route is chosen, the next decision has to do with the investment committee's ability to find these active managers. The decision to use active strategies takes up a significant amount of the investment committee members' time given the value-added delivered. Getting the best-in-class investment management organization is not as important as the consultants make it out to be—given the management organization's relatively low impact on total fund performance results.

- *Business Focus:* Investment management is a business, with revenues, costs, and profits. As a result, investment management firms are run as businesses. One of the most important questions to ask a money manager is how it is reinvesting in its business. Is it spending its profits (own money) on adding to the portfolio management team, to the marketing focus, to service capabilities, or to the infrastructure? Typically, when the capital reinvestment is intended to increase the number of professionals or add to their decision-making process, it is a sign that the firm is thinking longer term. If the monies go toward marketing, the firm might have changed its focus from managing portfolios to gathering assets. If the profits leave every night with the partners, it could mean that the firm is preparing itself for sale. Investment management is highly profitable—likely having the highest profit margins and return on capital of any other business.

- *Alignment of Interests:* The investment industry is driven by financial incentives. Some incentives are good (aligned with the best interests of the plan sponsor), and some are not so good (designed for self-interest). Unfortunately, most of the incentive programs created by the various service providers in dealing with plan sponsors are not effectively aligned with the client's best interests. As a result, the costs to manage the investment funds might be too high. Incentives come in all shapes and sizes. A good incentive structure is one that provides some pain to service providers that do not achieve the goals and objectives agreed upon.

Furthermore, the money manager should not earn an additional fee for doing the job it was hired to do in the first place.

- *Performance:* Historical investment performance results are not a predictor of future performance. This cannot be stated enough. However, given that qualitative assessments in evaluating money managers are difficult to judge, the only factor that is visible is historical performance—while it is not reliable, it can be measured. Firing money managers due to underperformance might not be in the fund's best interest (obviously, depending on the reasons for this underperformance). Historical performance is not the decisive criterion for hiring and firing a money manager; rather, it is how the *reason* for the performance came about.

- *Benchmarking:* Typically, the less efficient or concentrated the market in which the fund is invested, the less appropriate the index is as a benchmark for comparing performance results. Selecting an inappropriate benchmark is likely to result in unreliable data for measuring success. Furthermore, the less efficient the market, the greater the opportunity for the money manager to outperform.

- *Commission Allocation Policy:* Commission dollars are the property of the plan sponsor. The investment committee should take the time to lay out an effective commission directive policy.

- *Consultant Relationship:* There is no question that the role of the investment committee is important. Even with in-depth investment experience and knowledge on the committee, an independent sounding board from the outside is needed for trend updates within the investment and plan sponsor community. Hire a consultant so you have someone to blame if things go wrong.

- *Cost Controls:* Part of being prudent is focusing on the overall cost of the pension or investment program. Most plan sponsors pay way too much in fees, given the value that is created. Investment committee members are expected to achieve the goals and objectives within a cost framework that justifies the judgments made. It seems that focusing on overall costs in administering and managing pension and investment fund assets has a very low priority (if it is a priority at all).

The true bottom line: The investment committee should do whatever is required to increase the odds of success—acting in their fiduciary capacity for the plan beneficiaries. There is no substitute for prudence.

FINAL THOUGHTS

- The members of an investment committee should always seek out *consensus* rather than *compromise.*

- The investment committee members should be wary of anything that is free, or appears to be free—they may find that the cost is unaffordable.

- "All things being equal" is a phrase that does not apply to the investment field. Nothing is equal.

- Pretty much every decision regarding the administration and management of a pension or investment fund is built on "best guesses." And, since no one can predict the future, all decisions are basically a *hedge* against what could go wrong. Some of the best decisions an investment committee should make are sometimes contrary to current beliefs and human nature, and might not provide total comfort to the members.

- History has shown that there is not a lot of stability within the investment management community—regardless of whether the firms are large or small, public or private, and irrespective of the types of compensation schemes they have in place. The industry is always in a stage of flux.

- The plan sponsor community, the overseers of pension and investment funds, and money managers all would like brokerage firms to unbundle their commission charges. This would open the way for money managers and plan sponsors to determine the actual cost of transacting—to see the allocation between pure execution, servicing, and research (both proprietary and third-party). Yet money managers charge one bundled fee for all clients within the same mandate and with the same asset size—even though one client may require only one meeting a year while another may require four. The latter client may be located on the other side of the country (or even in another country) while the former client may be located within the same city. One client might be the recipient of entertainment from the manager, perhaps due to location, while another client might not. This is another way for one client to receive more favorable treatment from the money manager than another. If money managers were to unbundle their fee structure, their clients would be able to determine what they are willing to pay for. For example, if a client knew that four meetings a year from the money manager would cost them an extra 1 basis point in management fees, they might be willing to accept just one or two meetings a year. If a client knew that being entertained cost an extra 1 basis point a year in fees, it might be willing to skip the entertainment package. This could result in a win-win situation for the plan sponsor and the money management organization: the plan sponsor would receive a lower fee while the money manager would have lower costs—and perhaps the real benefit of treating all clients equally and fairly. Unbundling would help to level the playing field.

Just some thoughts.

APPENDICES

APPENDIX 1

CODE OF CONDUCT, ETHICS, AND CONFIDENTIALITY POLICY

PURPOSE

The investment committee seeks to fulfill its fiduciary role in accordance with the laws, codes, and standards of the relevant regulatory and governing authorities, accepted industry practices, and the highest standards of integrity and fair dealing.

PRINCIPLE

This policy sets out the fundamental standards of behavior expected of all members of the investment committee.

CODE OF CONDUCT

The members of the investment committee must always act in the best interests of plan beneficiaries. As a result, members must:

- ensure that they act in a prudent manner when overseeing all the activities as they relate to the investment fund;

- conduct themselves with integrity and dignity and act in an ethical manner;

- use their best efforts to avoid conflicts of interest and ensure fairness when selecting the various service providers to support the activities required by the investment fund;

- inform the plan sponsor of any activity or interest that might impair their ability to render unbiased and objective advice with any aspect of the investment fund; and,

- exercise diligence, thoroughness, and independent professional judgment in overseeing all investment activities.

ETHICS

The members of the investment committee must uphold the standards and values expected of a fiduciary responsible for the ongoing administration and management of the investment fund assets. The members of the investment committee will always act in a prudent manner with the care, due diligence, and integrity of a trustee responsible for the caretaking of the assets and property of others.

The members of the investment committee must place the interests of the beneficiaries before their own. As a result, the members have an obligation to seek out the various service providers that reflect the beliefs, mission, and values as outlined in our investment policy statement. Each member is personally responsible for ensuring that the decisions made within the investment committee are void of self-interest.

CONFLICTS OF INTEREST

To prevent and/or detect any conflicts of interest that may arise in the administration of the funds entrusted to the members of the investment committee, the following procedures have been established:

- *Disclosure of personal holdings and business activities:* Members of the investment committee must submit on an annual basis a certificate of compliance that includes disclosure of any directorships held, interests in or debts owed to any enterprise with which the plan sponsor has a business relationship, and any gifts, benefits, or favors received in connection with the performance of their business and personal responsibilities. Furthermore, members must fully disclose any relationship, financial or otherwise, between a member of the investment committee and any service provider supporting the function of the investment fund; any perceived potential conflicts of interest should be brought to the attention of the plan sponsor.

- *Preclearance of trades:* Members of the investment committee must seek and obtain written approval before conducting any public securities transactions for their own account or other investment accounts they have influence over.

- *Restricted list:* Trading in any securities by members of the investment committee in which the plan sponsor has or may have insider information is strictly prohibited.

CONFIDENTIALITY

All activities conducted and undertaken by the members of the investment committee, as well as all information gathered and reported to the members, must remain confidential in the best interests of all plan beneficiaries.

APPENDIX 2
INVESTMENT POLICY & PROCEDURES STATEMENT: OUTLINE

INTRODUCTION

- Nature of client
- Plan description
- Purpose of statement
- Beliefs
- Investment goals and objectives
- Timeframe
- Mission
- Liquidity requirements
- Beneficiaries
- Tax considerations
- Regulatory, legislative, and legal environment

INVESTMENT COMMITTEES

- Sub-committee of the board or external committee
  - Monitor internal committee activities
  - Review and approve policies
  - Review and approve manager selection
  - Monitor performance
  - Approve asset mix classes/allocation/rebalancing process

- Management Committee
  - Provide advice and make recommendations to the board or external committee
  - Monitor and evaluate existing managers
  - Monitor portfolio activity

  - Monitor and evaluate performance results
  - Recommend asset mix classes and allocation
  - Prepare and review policies
  - Recommend and select managers
  - Provide ongoing education

- Chief Investment Officer
  - Role
  - Authorities
  - Responsibilities
  - Reporting function

- Investment Staff
  - Review service providers' reports
  - Monitor fund activities
  - Propose pertinent reports
  - Monitor performance
  - Negotiate contracts

- Meetings
  - Agenda and topics
  - Frequency
  - Attendance

POLICIES

- Asset mix
- Proxy voting (responsibility/guidelines)
- Rebalancing
- Currency
- Pricing
- Soft dollar
- Broker selection/commission allocation
- Security lending
- Social responsibility

DIVERSIFICATION

- Criteria

GUIDELINES AND RESTRICTIONS

- Preferences
- Unique needs

PERFORMANCE STANDARDS

- Benchmark
- Value-added target
- Peer-group sample
- Time horizon
- Tolerance ranges

RISK TOLERANCE

- Ability
- Willingness
- Appetite

COMPLIANCE

- By whom
- Corrective measures

SERVICE PROVIDERS

- Investment managers
- Actuary
- Investment planning consultant
- Accountant
- Auditor
- Lawyer
- Custodian

- Performance measurer
- Broker

COST OVERSIGHT

- Ongoing evaluation

MONITORING

- Required reports

APPENDIX 3
U.S.: YEARLY RATES OF CHANGE

Capital Market - U.S.: Annual Rates of Return (1926 to 2020)

-50 to -40	-40 to -30	-30 to -20	-20 to -10	-10 to 0	0 to 10	10 to 20	20 to 30	30 to 40	40 to 50	50 to 60
1931	1937	1930	1941	1929	1947	1926	1942	1927	1928	1933
	2008	1974	1957	1932	1948	1944	1943	1936	1935	1954
		2002	1966	1934	1956	1949	1951	1938	1958	
			1973	1939	1960	1952	1961	1945		
			2001	1940	1970	1959	1963	1950		
				1946	1978	1964	1967	1955		
				1953	1984	1965	1976	1975		
				1962	1987	1968	1982	1980		
				1969	1992	1971	1983	1985		
				1977	1994	1972	1996	1989		
				1981	2005	1979	1998	1991		
				1990	2007	1986	1999	1995		
				2000	2011	1988	2003	1997		
					2015	1993	2009	2013		
					2018	2004	2017	2019		
						2006				
						2010				
						2012				
						2014				
						2016				
						2020				

Source: Standard & Poor's

APPENDIX 4
CANADA: YEARLY RATES OF CHANGE

Capital Market - Canada: Annual Rates of Return (1924 to 2020)

-40 to -30	-30 to -20	-20 to -10	-10 to 0	0 to 10	10 to 20	20 to 30	30 to 40	40 to 50	50 to 60
				2020					
				2017	2016				
				2014	2010				
				2013	2006	2019			
				2012	2004	2005			
				2007	1997	2003			
				2000	1995	1996			
				1987	1991	1989			
			2018	1986	1988	1985			
			2011	1982	1977	1978	2009		
			1998	1973	1976	1972	1999		
		2015	1994	1971	1975	1968	1993		
		2002	1992	1965	1967	1964	1983		
		2001	1984	1960	1963	1955	1980		
		1990	1970	1959	1956	1951	1961		
		1981	1969	1953	1948	1949	1958		
		1940	1966	1952	1944	1936	1954		
2008		1937	1962	1947	1943	1934	1945		
1931	1974	1932	1946	1941	1942	1926	1935	1979	1950
1930	1957	1929	1939	1938	1924	1925	1928	1927	1933

Source: Canadian Institute of Actuaries (1924 to 1955); Toronto Stock Exchange (1956 to present)

APPENDIX 5
INVESTMENT MANAGEMENT AGREEMENT: OUTLINE

PARTIES INVOLVED/CONTACT PERSONNEL

- Pension fund/investor
- Money manager
- Custodian
- Actuary
- Investment planning consultant

APPOINTMENT DATE

PLAN DETAIL

GOVERNING LAWS

SPECIFIC PORTFOLIO MANDATE

AUTHORITIES AND RESPONSIBILITIES

INVESTMENT VEHICLES

- Segregated/separate account
- Commingled/pooled fund

INVESTMENT GUIDELINES AND CONSTRAINTS

- Leverage
- Currency management
- Use of derivatives
- Eligible and ineligible securities

PORTFOLIO GOALS AND OBJECTIVES

- Return expectations (capital appreciation vs. income)
- Cash flow requirements
- Liquidity needs

PERFORMANCE STANDARDS

- Benchmark
- Value-added target
- Timeframe
- Peer-group sample
- Tolerance range

CONFIDENTIALITY

IMPLEMENTATION

TERMINATION

- Reasons
- Timeframe

FEES

- Schedule
- Calculation
- Incentive-based

REPORTING PROCEDURES

- Meeting frequency
- Required reports
- Agenda
- Attendance

DISPUTE PROCESS

DEFINITIONS

APPENDIX

- Investment policy statement
- Proxy voting policy
- Broker selection and commission allocation policy
- Security lending policy
- Soft-dollar policy

APPENDIX 6
TRADE AND BROKERAGE ALLOCATION POLICY: SAMPLE

PURPOSE

In dealings with the brokerage community, brokerage commissions are generated when security transactions occur. These commission dollars are the sole property of the plan sponsor. As a result, the allocation of commission dollars must be undertaken in the best interests of the plan beneficiaries.

PRINCIPLES

The members of the investment committee have a duty and obligation to ensure the quality of the transactions undertaken on behalf of the investment fund by:

- seeking to obtain "best execution";
- minimizing transaction costs; and
- using brokerage commissions to benefit the plan beneficiaries.

DEFINITIONS

Soft dollars are arrangements whereby the investment manager directs securities transactions to a brokerage firm in exchange for execution service and research—provided through either the brokerage firm or a third-party vendor.

Directed commission arrangements occur when the plan sponsor directs a trade, typically through an investment manager or the plan sponsor itself, if there is a special account set up, to pay for a service or specific research that directly benefits the plan beneficiaries.

Commission recapture programs are direct arrangements between a plan sponsor and a broker or a consultant, where a portion of the commission dollars paid is rebated to the investment fund and treated as income.

DELEGATION

Although the members of the investment committee are not in favor of soft-dollar transactions by the investment managers to third-party vendors, the members do realize that investment managers may require certain research, economic, political, and social information provided by these vendors and that falls outside the normal distribution channels. As a result, brokerage selection and commission allocation have been delegated as a responsibility of the investment manager.

REPORTING

The members of the investment committee receive a commission allocation report from the equity investment managers on an annual basis for review. This report includes a list of brokers in which commissions for the investment fund were generated, the percentage of commission dollars generated through each broker, and the split between commissions allocated to pure execution, the amount for internally generated research, and the amount allocated to third-party research. With third-party research, a description is given of the type of service provided and why it is considered valuable by the investment manager in its decision-making process for this investment fund.

APPENDIX 7
PROXY VOTING POLICY: SAMPLE

PURPOSE

One of the responsibilities of the plan sponsor in the ongoing administration and management of the investment fund for the benefit of all plan beneficiaries is the creation of shareholder value. One significant mechanism of good governance is the exercise of voting rights. The proxy vote is an important aspect of any investment portfolio.

DELEGATION

The plan sponsor delegates the responsibility for proxy voting to the equity investment managers within its investment management structure to optimize the long-term value of those securities held within the investment fund. The investment committee gives the money manager the authority, responsibility, and accountability to vote in favor of any proposal that, in its opinion, will enhance the value of the security held, and against any proposal that will reduce the value of the security or increase the risk of the portfolio beyond an acceptable limit. If the money manager believes that it or any of its investment professionals has any conflict or potential conflict of interest, then this should be brought to the attention of the investment committee members. After a thorough review, the investment committee members could delegate the money manager to vote based on its judgments; give full discretion to the custodian to vote on its behalf; seek outside counsel about how to vote the proxy; or vote the proxy themselves based on their own judgment.

The investment committee reviews the proxy voting report from its investment managers on an annual basis.

APPENDIX 8
INVESTMENT COMMITTEE MANDATE STATEMENT: OUTLINE

DELEGATION OF DUTIES

- By whom: the board of directors; the sub-committee of the board responsible for pension/investment oversight; government directed; the chief investment officer; the management team of the plan sponsor organization
- Kept or delegated authority and responsibilities
- Outlining beliefs (plan-related)
- Setting policies
- Accountability
- Risk tolerance/appetite
- Reporting processes and procedures
- Selection of pertinent external service providers

MISSION

- Determining the stakeholders
- Highlighting that various regulatory authorities with influence
- Reflecting plan characteristics
- Know the beneficiaries
- Select qualified service providers

MEMBERSHIP

- Qualifications
- Chairperson
- Number
- Voting members
- Term limit

RESPONSIBILITIES

- Outlining beliefs (investment related)
- Formulation of policies
- Risk management
- Fund oversight
  - Ensure ongoing compliance
  - Monitor and evaluate investment performance
  - Monitor and evaluate investment service providers
- Selection of money management firms
- Selection of other external service providers
- Remain up-to-date on pension and investment trends

MEETINGS

- Attendance
- Frequency
- Processes/procedures
- Time requirements
- Minutes
- Voting
- Reporting

APPENDIX 9

INVESTMENT MANAGEMENT EVOLUTION

	Pre-1960s	1960s	1970s	1980s	1990s	2000s and Beyond
Major Influences	• Institutional dominance • Relationship driven	• Institutions still dominate • Fee for service • Counseling firms embryonic	• Counseling firms emerge • Pension asset growth • First index fund • Modern portfolio theory • Security lending • Consultants	• Counseling firms dominate • Consultants emerge • Asset mix management • Liability-driven investing	• Greater competition • Globalization • Legislation/ regulation • Manager life-cycle issues • Slow cash flow growth • Social investing	• Choices • Consolidation • Differentiation • Pressure on fees • Outsourcing • Total return management • Growth in DC plans • Behavioral finance
Policy	• Manager driven • Market oriented	• Manager driven • Market oriented	• Manager driven • Market oriented	• Consultant driven • Liability driven	• Consultant driven • Liability driven	• Plan sponsor driven • Liability driven
Asset Classes	• Cash • Domestic stocks • Bonds • Term loans	• Mortgages	• Non-domestic equities (regional)	• Non-domestic equities (global) • Real estate • Venture capital	• Global equities • Mortgage-backed securities • Managed futures • Emerging markets • Small-cap stocks • Real return bonds	• Hedge funds • Private equity • Infrastructure • Commodities • High-yield bonds • Global fixed income • Distressed debt

Investment Approach	• Balanced • Buy/hold • Qualitative • Income driven	• Balanced • Active management	• Specialty emerges • Market timing	• Specialty growth • Multi-manager structure	• Specialization • Multi-manager structure • Tactical asset association • Portfolio insurance • Quantitative • Passive/indexation	• Specialization • Passive dominates • Currency management • Socially responsible investing • De-risking • Immunization/ dedication • Absolute return strategies
Investment Focus	• Concentrated	• Concentrated	• Diversification - asset class - manager type	• Diversification - asset class - manager type	• Diversification - asset class - manager type - investment style	• Diversification - asset class segment - investment style
Performance Standards	• Absolute - inflation + • Total fund	• Relative - peer group • Components	• Relative - peer group • Components	• Comparative - benchmark	• Comparative - benchmark	• Comparative - customized benchmark
Timeframe	• Long (10 years)	• Long (5–10 years)	• Medium (4 years)	• Medium (4 years)	• Medium (4 years)	• Short (1–3 years)